GEORGIA

DAILY DEVOTIONS FOR DIE-HARD FANS

BULLDOGS

GEORGIA

Library of Congress Cataloging-in-Publication Data
13 ISBN Digit ISBN: 978-0-9840847-1-5

Manufactured in the United States of America.

For bulk purchases or to request the author for speaking engagements, email slynn@extrapointpublishers.com.

Go to http://www.die-hardfans.com for information about other titles in the series.

Cover and interior design by Slynn McMinn.

BULLDOGS

For My Father & My Mother,
and Nelson Mitchell,
Dog Fans Eternal

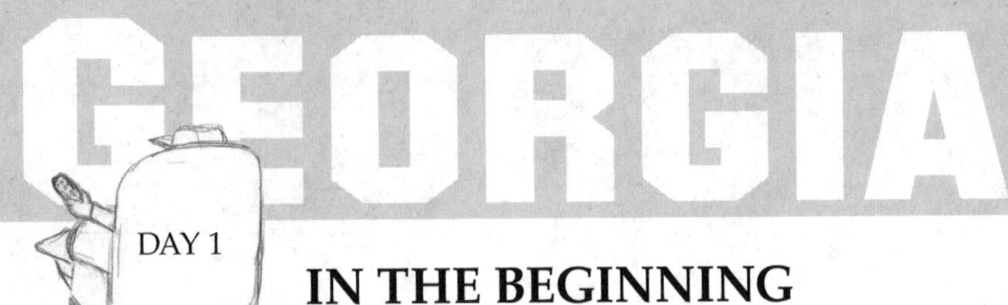

DAY 1

IN THE BEGINNING

Read Genesis 1, 2:1-3.

"God saw all that he had made, and it was very good" (v. 1:31).

Dr. Charles Herty simply threw a ball out onto a field and told the guys to go get it. Thus did football begin at the University of Georgia.

The "Father of Georgia football," Herty was an undergraduate at UGA in the 1880s. After classes each day on a bare and stubbly playing field behind New College, "the college boys gathered . . . running, jumping, scuffling, or just playing the fool." They had a football, but just sort of kicked it around.

When Dr. Herty returned to Athens in 1891 with his PhD to teach chemistry, the students were still romping aimlessly around. In Baltimore he had first seen football, "the craze of the East. He was immediately fascinated." He began to tell the students of the games he had seen, and they responded enthusiastically. The Glee Club gave $50 to remove rocks and fill up holes in the field. A pair up crude goalposts went up.

George Shackelford was at the first practice: "Dr. Herty simply tossed the football in the air and watched us scramble for it," he recalled. "He selected the strongest looking specimens for the first team."

Thin, bespectacled, and looking like anything but a football coach, Herty roused his players out of bed each morning for a three-mile run before breakfast and followed that with an ice-cold shower. In the afternoon, Herty gathered his players and taught them the rudiments of the new game, lecturing from a Walter Camp rule book he carried with him.

On Jan. 30, 1892, Georgia defeated Mercer 50-0 at the campus field, which later would be named Herty Field. It was the first intercollegiate football game in the Deep South.

Beginnings are important, but what we make of them is even more important. Consider, for example, how far the University of Georgia football program has come since Dr. Herty tossed out that first ball.

Every morning, you get a gift from God: a new beginning. God hands to you as an expression of divine love a new day full of promise and the chance to right the wrongs in your life. You can use the day to pay a debt, start a new relationship, replace a burned-out light bulb, tell your family you love them, chase a dream, solve a nagging problem . . . or not.

God simply provides the gift. How you use it is up to you. People often talk wistfully about starting over or making a new beginning. God gives you the chance with the dawning of every new day. You have the chance today to make things right – and that includes your relationship with God.

The most important key to achieving great success is to decide upon your goal and launch, get started, take action, move.

-- John Wooden

Every day is not just a dawn; it is a precious chance to start over or begin anew.

DAY 2

A SECOND CHANCE

Read John 7:53-8:11.

"'Then neither do I condemn you,' Jesus declared. 'Go now and leave your life of sin'" (v. 8:11).

Mike Bobo needed a chance for redemption. He got it in one of the most spectacular Bulldog wins of all time.

Bobo, whom Mark Richt named his offensive coordinator in 2006, is one of Georgia's greatest quarterbacks, ranking first, second, or third in seven different offensive categories. He started the first nine games in 1996, his junior year, but the season came unraveled, and the Dogs limped into Auburn to take on the 20th-ranked Tigers only 3-5. Bobo was benched.

Georgia was thoroughly whipped most of the game, trailing 28-7 before Bobo got a second chance and led one of the greatest comebacks in UGA history. The Dogs scored three touchdowns in the fourth quarter, the last one among Georgia's most dramatic scores ever. With third and 18 at the Auburn 31 with only one second left, Bobo "threw a prayer to the right front corner of the end zone. It was answered by sophomore Corey Allen. . . for a miraculous touchdown," the first of his career.

When Hap Hines kicked the extra point to tie the score, the stage was set for the SEC's first-ever overtime game. Torin Kirtsey scored on a one-yard run in the fourth overtime, and then Jason Ferguson and Brandon Tolbert stopped the Auburn quarterback short on fourth and three. The Dogs had a 56-49 win.

Bobo had a spectacular game, completing 21 of 37 passes for 360 yards and two touchdowns, a 67-yarder to Hines Ward and the miracle to Allen. Ward called him "the rejuvenated Bobo." "It's the best feeling I've ever had," Bobo said, "the biggest win of my life."

Mike Bobo achieved his redemption.

"If I just had a second chance, I know I could make it work out." Ever said that? If only you could go back and tell your dad one last time you love him, take that job you passed up rather than relocate, or marry someone else. If only you had a second chance, a mulligan.

As the story of Jesus' encounter with the adulterous woman illustrates, with God you always get a second chance. No matter how many mistakes you make, God will never give up on you. Nothing you can do puts you beyond God's saving power. You always have a second chance because with God your future is not determined by your past or who you used to be. It is determined by your relationship with God through Jesus Christ.

God is ready and willing to give you a second chance – or a third chance or a fourth chance – if you will give him a chance.

I have to thank God for giving me the gift that he did as well as a second chance for a better life.

-- Olympics figure skating champion Oksana Baiul

You get a second chance with God if you give him a chance.

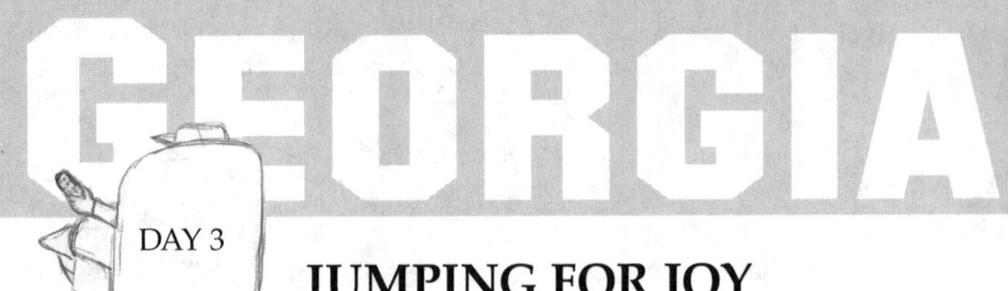

JUMPING FOR JOY

Read Luke 6:20-26.

"Rejoice in that day and leap for joy, because great is your reward in heaven" (v. 23).

Wilt Chamberlain, who knew a thing or two about dunking a basketball, once said the greatest dunker he ever saw was a "white boy who played for Atlanta around 1970." That "white boy" was UGA's own Herb White.

A native of Decatur, White was a three-year letterman for the Dogs, who started at forward in 1970, his senior year, and averaged 9.8 points and 6.4 rebounds for Coach Ken Rosemond's 13-12 team. Perhaps he became most familiar to Georgians over the years as one of the faces and voices of Georgia Public Television's frequent fundraising campaigns.

White was drafted in the eighth round by the Atlanta Hawks. Selected as a back-up for Pete Maravich, he not surprisingly saw limited action, playing only one season, getting into 38 games, and averaging 2.4 points and 1.3 rebounds. That's not much chance to gain a reputation as a world-class dunker, let alone earn his nickname, the "Elevator from Decatur."

White's fame, though, came from pre-game layup drills. As Chamberlain put it, White "never got off the bench, but in warm-ups he could dunk better than anyone I've ever seen." White said, "You got to know who the dunkers were, and by the end of the year, everyone pretty much agreed that Claude English [of the

Portland Trailblazers] and me were the two best." The two faced off before a game in Atlanta in April 1971 to determine the NBA's best dunker. English did a one-handed 360, "a dunk I could do with two balls," White said. White then pulled off a two-handed 360 and English conceded.

You're probably a pretty good jumper yourself when Georgia scores against Florida, Tennessee, or Auburn. You just can't help it. It's like your feet and your seat have suddenly become magnets that repel each other. The sad part is that you always come back down to earth; the moment of exultation passes.

But what if you could jump for joy all the time? Not literally, of course; you'd pass out from exhaustion. But figuratively, with your heart aglow and joyous even when life is its most difficult.

Joy is an absolutely essential component of the Christian life. Not only do we experience joy in our public praise and worship – which is temporary – but we live daily in the joy that comes from the presence of God in our lives and the surety of his saving power extended to us through Jesus Christ.

It's not happiness, which derives from external factors; it's joy, which comes from inside.

No one can say 'You must not run faster than this, or jump higher than that.' The human spirit is indomitable.

-- Sir Roger Bannister, first to run a sub-4-minute mile

Unbridled joy can send you jumping all over the place; life in Jesus means such exultation is not rare but rather is a way of life.

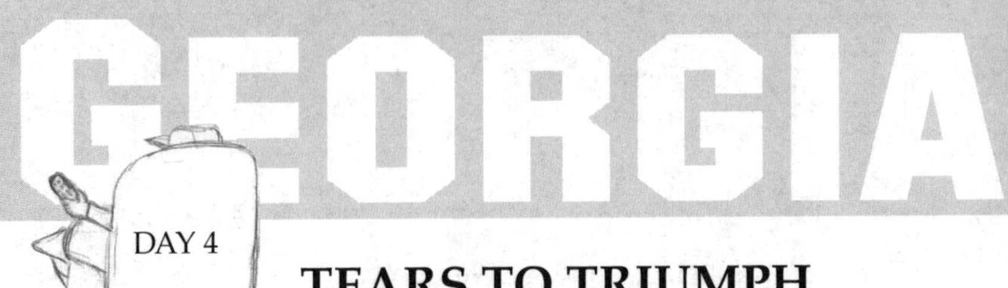

TEARS TO TRIUMPH

Read Matthew 27:45--61.

"Many women were there, watching from a distance. They had followed Jesus from Galilee to care for his needs" (v. 55).

They used to boo him. But not any more.

John Lastinger started at quarterback for Georgia in 1982 and '83, and the Dogs went 20-2-1 in those games. The undefeated 1982 team played Penn State in the Sugar Bowl for the national championship. Lastinger's general play, however, was not among the bright spots. As he put it, Terry Hoage was the star of the Georgia highlight tape for the 1982 Vanderbilt game, and "I was the star of the Vanderbilt tape. I was that bad."

After the 1983 Clemson game, Lastinger was benched. When he went in against South Carolina to replace the injured starter, Todd Williams, the Georgia fans booed him. They booed him again when the second half started.

Lastinger started the rest of the season as the Dogs lost only to Auburn 13-7. Then in the Cotton Bowl against heavily favored and second-ranked Texas came one of those glorious moments in Georgia football history.

Georgia trailed 9-3 with less than three minutes to play when Lastinger scored from 17 yards out on one of the most famous runs in Bulldog history. Georgia won 10-9. "I just remember my teammates grabbing me. I was thinking that so many players have had their Georgia moments and maybe now I had mine," Lastinger recalled.

Decades later, he said, "It is still fun to to back to Athens. When they say my name at the stadium now, people cheer and I smile. I remember there was a time when they didn't do that."

The jeers have turned to cheers—the tears to triumph.

We all have times of defeat and loss in our lives, but nothing fills us with such an overwhelming sense of helplessness as the death of a loved one. There's absolutely nothing you can do about it. Like the women who stood at a distance and watched Jesus die on the darkest, bleakest day in history, you, too, can only stand helpless and weep as something precious and beautiful leaves your life.

For the believer in Jesus Christ and his loved ones, though, the Sunday of resurrection – the grandest, most triumphant day in history – follows the Friday of death. Faith in Jesus transforms loss into triumph, not only for the loved one but for those left behind.

Amid your tears and your sense of loss, you celebrate the ultimate victory of your family member or friend. Amid death, you find life; amid sorrow, you find hope.

What a way to die! What a way to live!

The triumph cannot be had without the struggle.
– Olympic Gold Medalist Wilma Rudolph

Faith in Jesus Christ transforms death from the ultimate defeat to the ultimate victory.

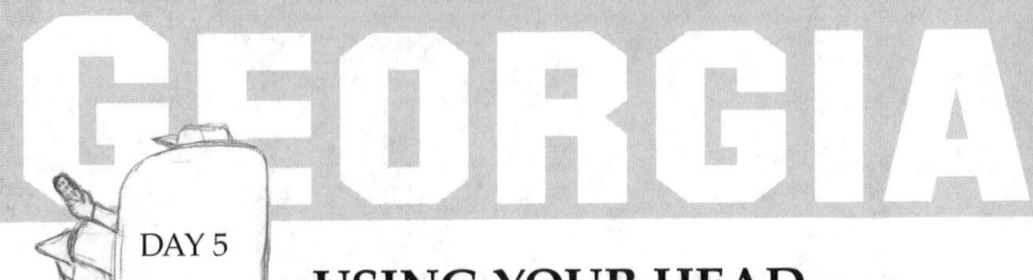

USING YOUR HEAD

Read Job 28.

"The fear of the Lord -- that is wisdom, and to shun evil is understanding" (v. 28).

George "Kid" Woodruff used his head to win football games as a coach for the Dogs, but he once used his head – and his head-gear – to win a game as a player.

A successful businessman, Woodruff coached for five seasons, from 1923-27, for $1 a year. He didn't want the job but was the "overwhelming" choice of school officials and couldn't turn his alma mater down in a time of need. He compiled a 30-16-1 record, and his 1927 team was the first in school history to win nine games in a season.

As a player in 1907, Woodruff actually got some unexpected coaching experience. In the Tech game that season, Coach W.S. Whitney used five players who weren't Georgia students, paying them $150 plus expenses. As they left town, the players confessed, and the stunt cost Whitney his job. Whitney denied paying the men any money, but confessed he "naturally knew" they had played football elsewhere and "did not search into the details of obtaining them." When Whitney's assistant coach was banned from the bench, the team didn't have a coach for the Auburn game. So Woodruff took over, quarterbacking Georgia to a 6-0 upset.

His most famous bit of innovation came against Sewanee in

1911, a unique twist on the classic Statue of Liberty play. As a thick Tennessee fog rolled across the field, Woodruff dropped back to pass, removed his headgear, and sailed it downfield. He then handed the ball to his halfback. In the fog, the Sewanee players chased the helmet instead of the ball while the halfback raced untouched for a touchdown. Georgia won 12-3.

You're a thinking person. When you talk about using your head, you're speaking as George "Kid" Woodruff did against Sewanee with his quick thinking that took advantage of the situation. Logic and reason are part of your psyche. A coach's bad call frustrates you and your children's inexplicable behavior flummoxes you. Why can't people just think things through?

That goes for matters of faith too. Jesus doesn't tell you to turn your brain off when you walk into a church or open the Bible. In fact, when you seek Jesus, you seek him heart, soul, body, and mind. The mind of the master should be the master of your mind so that you consider every situation in your life through the critical lens of the mind of Christ. With your head and your heart, you encounter God, who is, after all, the true source of wisdom.

To know Jesus is not to stop thinking; it is to start thinking divinely.

Football is more mental than physical, no matter how it looks from the stands.

-- Pro Hall-of-Fame linebacker Ray Nitschke

Since God is the source of all wisdom, it's only logical that you encounter him with your mind as well as your emotions.

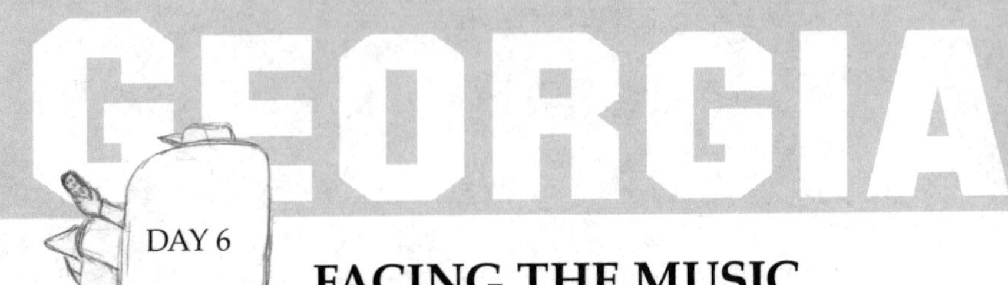

FACING THE MUSIC

Read Psalm 98.

"Sing to the Lord a new song, for he has done marvelous things" (v. 1).

If it's game day at Sanford Stadium it must be noisy, and the most raucous noisemakers of them all will be a group that began with twenty military cadets: The University of Georgia Redcoat Band.

The band started in 1905 as part of the Military Department, making its first non-military appearance at the 1906 Georgia-Clemson baseball game. The band early on played "Glory Glory to Old Georgia," composed by Hugh Hodgson, a former bandsman and later head of the school's music department. The Georgia fight song, incidentally, is not based on "Battle Hymn of the Republic," but rather on "John Brown's Body."

During the 1920s and 1930s, the band allowed some non-military musicians to join its ranks and began to make some trips with the football team. A train trip to Columbus for the Auburn game required raising $700, a project accomplished largely through the efforts of that new campus phenomenon called coeds.

Perhaps the seminal event in the band's history occurred during the 1935 football season when Georgia played LSU, which featured the "Golden Band from Tigerland," one of the largest marching bands in the nation. When alumni and school athletic officials saw the small Georgia contingent against the massive

LSU band, their embarrassment led to increased funding and more members.

The Redcoat Band as we know it today was born in 1955 with the arrival of Roger and Phyllis Dancz, who expanded it and created the Georgettes, who are the dance line, and the Georgia Flag Line, originally called the Bulldog Banners. Now about 375 musicians strong, the Georgia Redcoat Band is one of the nation's premier collegiate marching bands.

Maybe you can't play a lick or carry a tune in the proverbial bucket. Or perhaps you do know your way around a guitar or a keyboard and can sing "Georgia on My Mind" on karaoke night without closing the joint down.

Unless you're a professional musician, however, how well you play or sing really doesn't matter. What counts is that you have music in your heart and sometimes you have to turn it loose.

Worshipping God has always included music in some form. That same boisterous and musical enthusiasm you exhibit when the Redcoat Band gets to rocking and rolling after a Bulldog touchdown should be a part of the joy you have in your personal worship of God.

When you consider that God loves you, he always will, and he has arranged through Jesus for you to spend eternity with him, how can that song God put in your heart not burst forth?

I like it because it plays old music.

-- Pitcher Tug McGraw on his '54 Buick

You call it music; others may call it noise; God calls it praise.

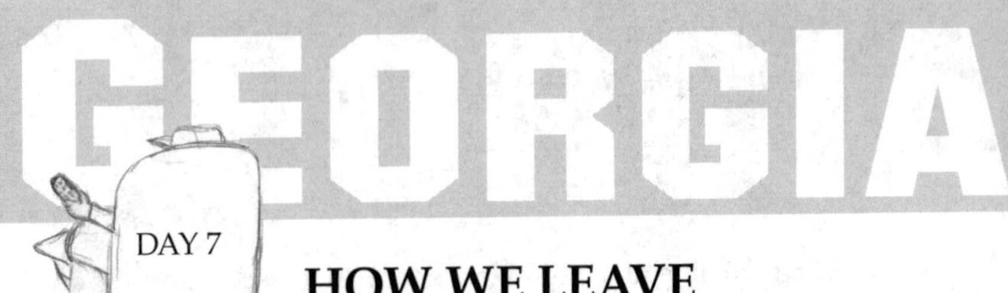

DAY 7

HOW WE LEAVE

Read 2 Kings 2:1-12.

"A chariot of fire and horses of fire appeared and separated the two of them, and Elijah went up to heaven in a whirlwind" (v. 11).

We can't always choose when we leave, but we can usually choose how we leave.

Johnny Griffith never really stood a chance. He followed the legendary Wally Butts when he was named Georgia head football coach after the 1960 season. He was coach of the freshmen at Georgia with no experience as a head coach in the SEC.

Moreover, Butts' resignation divided the alumni as to his successor. Vince Dooley said of the coach he succeeded, Griffith "had no opportunity. There was too much of a rift with the Georgia people, and there was not a person on the face of the earth who could have healed the split that existed from 1961 to 1963." After three losing seasons and a 10-16-4 record, Griffith resigned with a year left on his contract when Athletic Director Joel Eaves would not extend his contract.

"I know it was tough for him, a Georgia man, to go through what he went through," Dooley said of Griffith. So how did the outgoing coach handle the situation with the incoming coach? As Dooley said, "If he had gotten mad and skipped town, I surely wouldn't have blamed him."

But Griffith's behavior was "just the opposite." He did all he could to help the new staff, reviewing the current players and even helping out with recruiting. Griffith went so far as to accompany Dooley to Cedartown and sit with him in the stands to watch a recruit, Edgar Chandler, who would be an All-American guard at Georgia.

Johnny Griffith didn't really choose when he left, but he did decide to exit with style, grace, and class.

You probably haven't always chosen the moves you've made in your life. Perhaps your company transferred you. A landlord didn't renew your lease. An elderly parent needed your care.

Sometimes the only choice we have about leaving is the manner in which we go, whether we depart with style and grace or not. Our exit from life is the same way. Unless we usurp God's authority over life and death, we can't choose how we die, just how we handle it.

Perhaps the most frustrating aspect of dying is that we have at most very little control over the process. As with our birth, our death is in God's hands. We finally must surrender to his will even if we have spent a lifetime refusing to do so.

We do, however, control our destination. How we leave isn't up to us; where we spend eternity is -- and that depends on our relationship with Jesus.

Johnny Griffith showed a lot of class in that situation.
-- Vince Dooley on his predecessor

When you go isn't up to you; where you go is.

RUN FOR IT

Read John 20:1-10.

"Peter and the other disciple started for the tomb. Both were running, but the other disciple outran Peter and reached the tomb first" (vv. 3-4).

Today's UGA students entering the Tate Student Center may vaguely recall that Dean William Tate was a longtime faculty member and Dean of Men – but probably very few of them will know that in his prime "Wild Bill" Tate was one of the South's best distance runners.

Tate's prime was the 1920s, and even while he was at Georgia, his success as a distance runner resulted in high school runners across the state idolizing him in hopes of equaling his achievements. While he was in high school in Macon, Bob Young, who would later be conference champion at UGA, wrote Tate for advice on how to run the mile. For a while, Tate gladly helped out the young runner by sending him tips and instructions on a postcard each week.

Shortly after the correspondence began, to their surprise the teacher and his pupil met in Birmingham in the Southern Amateur Athletic Union mile race. The race was a classic with Tate and Young matching each other stride for stride for three laps until the high school runner put on a burst of speed and beat Tate to the tape.

Tate's coach was the legendary Herman Stegeman for whom

Stegeman Coliseum is named, and the dismayed coach ran up to his star miler and exclaimed, "What happened? How could you lose to this high school boy?" Tate replied, "Well, I guess he just had a smarter coach than I did."

Hit the ground running -- every morning that's what you do as you leave the house and re-enter the rat race. You run errands, you run though a presentation; you give someone a run for his money; you always want to be in the running and never run-of-the-mill.

You're always running toward something, such as your goals, or away from something, such as your past. Many of us spend much of our lives foolhardily attempting to run away from God, the purposes he has for us, and the blessings he is waiting to give us.

No matter how hard or how far you run, though, you can never outrun yourself or God. God keeps pace with you, calling you in the short run to take care of the long run by falling to your knees and running for your life -- to Jesus -- just as Peter and the other disciple ran that first Easter morning.

On your knees, you run all the way to glory.

I never get tired of running. The ball ain't that heavy.

-- Herschel Walker

You can run to eternity by going to your knees.

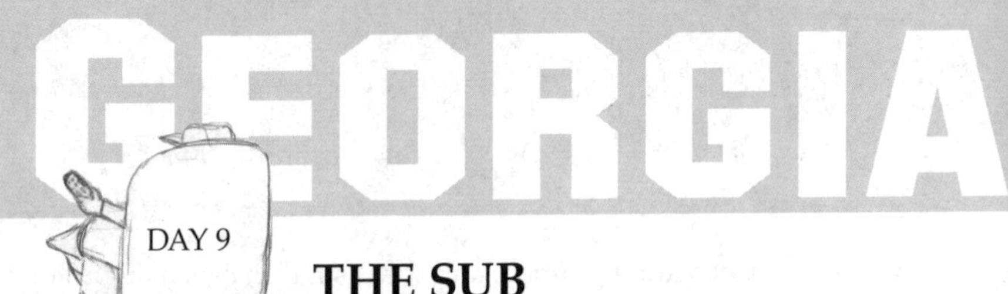

THE SUB

Read Galatians 3:10-14.

"Christ redeemed us from the curse of the law by becoming a curse for us" (v. 13).

On Oct. 31, 1970, Georgia pulled off the greatest comeback in its football history at that time – with its third string quarterback.

A national TV audience was as surprised as the Bulldog Nation was when South Carolina jumped out to a 21-3 lead in the second quarter. The situation looked grim for the Dogs, and it wasn't just the scoreboard that gave cause for concern. Both Georgia's number-one quarterback, Mike Cavan, and the player he had replaced, James Ray, were sidelined with injuries.

That left the Dawgs in the hands of the sub's sub: number-three quarterback Paul Gilbert, a senior from Athens. Gilbert had begun the 1988 season as the starting quarterback, but a broken leg in the first game seemed to send him permanently to the bench. On this day, though, he stepped forward to give one of the finest performances ever by a substitute player.

He hit Billy Brice and Charley Whittemore with long passes to set up Georgia's first touchdown. Gilbert then hit four passes on a drive and scored on an 11-yard run. He engineered an 81-yard, 18-play drive to start the third quarter, scoring from the one, and hit Brice with a 60-yard touchdown pass to put Georgia ahead for the first time.

South Carolina answered with a field goal and a 34-32 lead,

but they were finished and Gilbert wasn't. He hit Jimmy Shirer for 41 yards to set up his own 10-yard scoring run, and Georgia was not to be headed again.

Georgia won the offensive shoot-out going away 52-34, and Paul Gilbert the substitute scored three touchdowns rushing and passed for 245 yards.

Wouldn't it be cool if you had a substitute like Paul Gilbert for all life's hard stuff? Telling of a death in the family? Call in your sub. Breaking up with your boyfriend? Job interview? Chemistry test? Crucial presentation at work? Let the sub handle it.

We do have such a substitute, but not for the matters of life. Instead, Jesus is our substitute for matters of life and death. Since Jesus has already made it, we don't have to make the sacrifice God demands for forgiveness and salvation.

One of the ironies of our age is that many people desperately grope for a substitute for Jesus. Mysticicm, human philosophies such as Scientology, false religions such as Hinduism and Islam, cults, New Age approaches that preach self-fulfillment without responsibility or accountability – they and others like them are all pitiful, inadequate substitutes for Jesus.

Accept no substitutes. It's Jesus or nothing.

I never substitute just to substitute. The only way a guy gets off the floor is if he dies.

-- Former basketball coach Abe Lemons

There is no substitute for Jesus,
the consummate substitute.

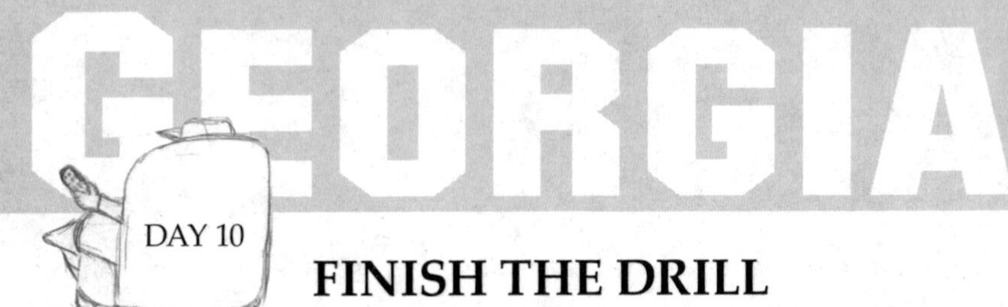

FINISH THE DRILL

Read Mark 14:32-42.

"'Father,' he said, 'everything is possible for you. Take this cup from me. Yet not what I will, but what you will'" (v. 36).

Finish the drill.

It became the catchphrase for the early years of the Mark Richt era at UGA. For 20 years, the Bulldogs had been unable to finish the drill by winning an SEC championship. Several times they had come close and faltered. On Nov. 16, 2002, at Auburn, they had yet another chance to finish after getting themselves into position with a 13-7 win at South Carolina and a last-minute 26-24 win over sixth-ranked Tennessee.

So how did the Dogs respond to the opportunity that lay before them? They went out and played what quarterback David Greene described as "an absolutely brutal first half. . . . There we were with everything on the line and we were just getting it handed to us."

The Dogs cut the 14-3 halftime deficit to 21-17 and got the ball with 1:58 left at their own 41. They had one last chance to finish the drill.

On the second play, Greene hit Fred Gibson all the way to the Auburn 14. But three incomplete passes and a five-yard penalty left the Dogs with one last gasp. "Greene took the snap, pump-faked toward Gibson on the right side, and lofted the ball. . . .

[Michael] Johnson leaped high and made his twelfth catch of the night, outreaching the smaller Auburn defender" for the touchdown. "It was just pitch and catch," Johnson would later say.

But the Bulldog Nation knew it was much more than that. It was a play that finished the drill. The Dogs were on their way to Atlanta and the SEC championship they claimed with a 30-3 rout of Arkansas.

Life is tough; it inevitably beats us up and kicks us around some. But life has four quarters, and so here we are, still standing, still in the game. Like the Bulldogs of 2002, we know that we can never win if we don't finish. We emerge as champions and winners only if we never give up, if we just see it through.

Interestingly, Jesus has been in the same situation. On that awful night in the garden, Jesus understood the nature of the suffering he was about to undergo, and he begged God to take it from him. In the end, though, he yielded to God's will and surrendered his own.

Even in the matter of persistence, Jesus is our example. As he did, we finish the drill – following God's will for our lives -- no matter how hard it gets. And we can do it because God is with us.

Never give up and sit down and grieve. Find another way.

– Satchel Paige

It's tough to keep going no matter what, but you have the power of almighty God to help pull you through.

TOUGH LOVE

Read Mark 10:17-22.

"Jesus looked at him and loved him. 'One thing you lack,' he said. 'Go, sell everything you have and give to the poor, and you will have treasure in heaven. Then come, follow me.' At this the man's face fell. He went away sad, because he had great wealth" (vv. 21-22).

Suzanne Yoculan once kicked one of her best gymnasts off the team -- and saved her life.

In the fall of 1990, Kelly Macy won the NCAA individual bars championship and was named the SEC's Freshman-of-the-Year. When the season ended, Macy determined to get stronger and better by losing some weight, and with her characteristic intensity, she did through severely restricting what she ate and vigorously working out. "Not one time," Macy said, "did it cross my mind that I was hurting myself."

But when Macy returned to Georgia in the fall, she was so weak she couldn't even do a handstand on bars -- and this was the bars national champion. She was down to about 80 pounds, and the coaches realized something was seriously wrong.

Yoculan told Macy that if she didn't start eating, she was off the team, that her father would come and take her home. When Macy insisted she didn't have a problem, Yoculan responded by basically kicking her off the team. Until she weighed 105 pounds, Macy had to come to the gym every day, eat a meal in front of

Yoculan, and watch everyone else work out. Even after Macy gained the lost weight back, Yoculan refused to let her move out of the athletic dormitory as gymnasts customarily did before their junior season. She wanted to monitor Macy's eating.

Macy said she didn't know what would have happened had not Yoculan given her "the wake-up call." Macy's parents knew, though; her dad said Yoculan's tough-love approach saved his daughter's life.

Expect your children to abide by your rules? The immediate reward you receive may be an intense and loud "I hate you," a flounce, and a slammed door. So why do it? Because you're the parent; you love your children, and you want them to become responsible adults. It's tough love.

Jesus also hands out tough love as the story of the young man illustrates. Jesus broke his heart, but the failure was in the young man, who despite his asseverations of devotion, loved his wealth more than he did Jesus.

Jesus is tough on us, too, in that he expects us to follow him no matter what it costs us. A well-executed flounce won't change anything either. As a parent does for his willful children, Jesus knows what is best for us. We'll appreciate that tough love with all our heart and soul on that glorious day when Jesus welcomes us to the place he has prepared for us.

The sterner the discipline, the greater the devotion.

– Basketball coach Pete Carill

Jesus expects us to do what he has told us to do — but it's because he loves us and wants the best for us in life and through eternity.

BLIND JUSTICE

Read Micah 6:6-8.

"He has showed you, O man, what is good. And what does the Lord require of you? To act justly and to love mercy and to walk humbly with your God" (v. 8).

What happened to the Lady Bulldogs in 1992 may still be the greatest injustice the NCAA selection committee has ever pulled off.

The Georgia women finished the season 19-11 and ranked No. 24 in the country. On the team were All-SEC player Lady Hardmon and the Lowe twins, Camille and Miriam. The 19 wins included victories over teams ranked No. 12 and No. 3 at the time and a trip to the finals of the SEC tournament. And yet they were left out of the field of 48 for the NCAA Tournament for the first time in history.

An infuriated and disbelieving coach Andy Landers called the selection process and the omission of his team "a joke, a total joke." He pointed to Vanderbilt's selection as the No. 3 seed in the East Regional; they lost twice to the Lady Dogs. Alabama finished behind the Lady Dogs in the SEC and in the tournament; yet the Tide got in. "What criteria?" Landers thundered. "The criteria is whatever they decide to say it is."

Saying, "I better not touch that,' Landers avoided pointing out that the head of the selection committee was the associate athletics director at UCLA, which made the tournament with a

19-9 record and an unranked team. He could have noted, too, that five Pac-10 teams were selected, though only one was ranked in the top 25.

Sportswriter Ailene Voisin assessed the situation succinctly: "No Lady Bulldogs. . . . No justice."

The Lady Dogs were done wrong.

Where's the justice when cars fly past you just as a state trooper pulls you over? When a con man swindles an elderly neighbor? When crooked politicians treat your tax dollars as their personal slush fund? When children starve?

Injustice enrages us, but anger is not enough. The establishment of justice in this world has to start with each one of us. The Lord requires it of us. For most of us, a just world is one in which everybody gets what he or she deserves.

But that is not God's way. God expects us to be just and merciful in all our dealings without consideration as to whether the other person "deserves" it. The justice we dispense should truly be blind.

If that doesn't sound "fair," then pause and consider that when we stand before God, the last thing we want is what we deserve. We want mercy, not justice.

None of us wants justice from God. What we want is mercy because if we got justice, we'd all go to hell.

-- Bobby Bowden

God requires that we dispense justice and mercy without regards to deserts, exactly what we pray we will in turn receive from God.

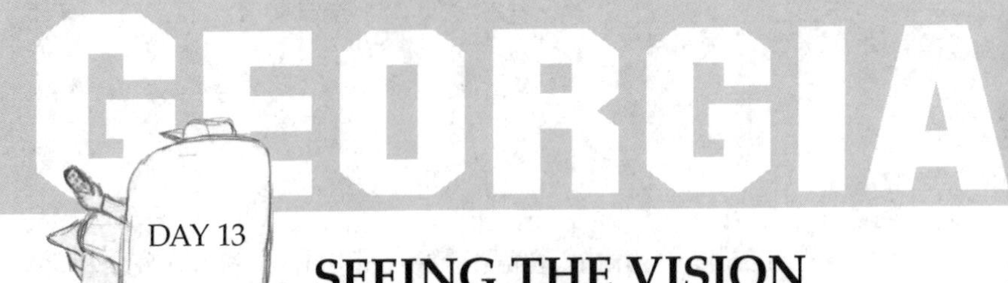

SEEING THE VISION

Read Acts 26:1, 9-23.

"So then, . . . I was not disobedient to the vision from heaven" (v. 19).

Steadman Sanford was a visionary.

Surely every Georgia football fan knows of Herschel and Garrison and Frank Sinkwich and Davids Greene and Pollack. But many Dawg fans probably file into Sanford Stadium knowing little about the man for whom the most beautiful college football stadium in the country is named.

Professor Sanford founded UGA's journalism school, but his vision encompassed sports as well as athletics. As faculty chairman of athletics, he championed the construction in 1910 of a new facility for both football and baseball, which the students insisted be named Sanford Field. By the 1920s, though, the little field couldn't handle the crowds that turned out for football games, forcing Georgia to play its biggest games on the road every year. "Every athletic contest should be played on the college campus," Sanford once said. "Athletics belong to the students on campus."

One spring day in 1925, Sanford stood atop a hill and looked down into a gully. The area was so steeply sloped and so thickly wooded that the only use the university could find for it was as a firing range for the rifle team. John Stegeman called it "a wild bottomland, a picturesque but marshy dale" and "a damp and shadowy valley." But UGA's great visionary saw something else.

As he stood there, Sanford told a student, "Someday there will be a great and beautiful stadium on this very site. It's a natural."

When Sanford first presented his idea of a great stadium in that natural amphitheater, the athletics board voted against him. His vision won out, though – and became the reality Sanford Stadium is today.

To speak of visions is often to risk their being lumped with palm readings, Ouija boards, seances, horoscopes, and other such useless mumbo-jumbo. The danger such mild amusements pose, however, is very real in that they indicate a reliance on something other than God. It is God who knows the future; it is God who has a vision and a plan for your life. A medium should be a steak and nothing more.

You probably do have a vision for your life, a plan for how it should unfold. It's the dream you pursue through your family, your job, your hobbies, your interests. But your vision inspires a fruitful life only if it is compatible with God's plan. As the apostle Paul found out, you ignore God's vision at your peril. But if you pursue it, you'll find an even more glorious life than you could ever have envisioned for yourself.

Professor Sanford wasn't interested so much in the beauty of the scene as with a vision that was haunting him: a natural bowl with a football field in the hollow.

-- John F. Stegeman

Your grandest vision for the future pales beside the vision God has of what the two of you can accomplish together.

THE SNAKE PIT

Read Matthew 23:29-39.

"You snakes! You brood of vipers! How will you escape being condemned to hell?" (v. 33)

Dan Magill has been called "probably the most influential man in the history of college tennis," but he once gained a measure of notoriety as the promoter of "The Big Snake Fight."

Back in the 1930s, before Magill began 34 years of coaching men's tennis at UGA and won more matches than any coach in collegiate history, he "had the brainstorm to put on a king snake-rattlesnake fight for the 'snake championship of the world.'" He had captured a six-foot king snake by a creek in Oconee County, and a good friend had snared a five-foot timber rattler.

In the local paper, Magill touted the "big snake fight" at the UGA tennis courts at high noon on Saturday. Admission was ten cents. A pretty good crowd of 200 or so showed up. Magill built a wooden ring and served as the announcer and the referee for the battle between Rastus Rattlesnake and Casper King Snake. He ended the introductions with "you snakes know the rules, at the sound of the whistle, come out fighting." Magill blew the whistle – and nothing happened. The two snakes just sat in their opposite corners, occasionally flicking their tongues.

The crowd began to yell for its money back, so Magill prodded the snakes to get some action going. The rattler promptly struck with such ferocity that Magill "jumped at least five feet in the air and plum out of the ring, barely escaping his fangs." The crowd cheered and, placated by Magill's frantic leap to safety, quit asking for a refund.

But the snakes never did fight.

Who would want to be known as a snake-in-the-grass? Or to be so unlucky, you're snake bit? Don't roll snake eyes if you're foolish enough to gamble, and don't drink any snake oil for medicinal help.

Snakes and mankind have never exactly been bosom buddies. The Old Testament often uses snakes (and serpents) as metaphors for something or someone who is dangerous and wicked. Thus, Jesus had a great scriptural tradition undergirding his referring to religious leaders as snakes.

Jesus' point was that the religious folks were wicked and dangerous because they appeared faithful and righteous on the outside while their hearts were not committed to the truth of the scripture they supposedly taught. That is, they failed to see Jesus for the savior he was and were leading their people to do the same, thus condemning them all to hell.

The insult still has meaning today, and God still has an awful fate reserved for the wicked snakes who turn their back on Jesus.

As soon as you think you are on top of the world, some snake comes out of the tall grass and cuts you down.

– NBA Hall of Famer Bill Russell

Snakes are the "almost" Christians, the ones for whom faithfulness is an external show that doesn't reach their hearts.

DAY 15

DREAM WORLD

Read Joel 2:26-28.

"Your old men will dream dreams, your young men will see visions" (v. 28).

Dreams can come true; sometimes it just takes a while. Kelley Hester needed seven years to land her dream job.

Hester was a three-time All-SEC golfer at Georgia in the 1990s, playing on the SEC champions of 1993 and 1994. She graduated in 1996, played on the Futures Tour, and worked as an assistant pro before she returned to Athens in 1999 as an assistant golf coach.

The 2000 season was Beans Kelly's last as head coach of the women's golf team, and Hester applied for the job. "It's just where I always wanted to be," she said. With only one year of collegiate head coaching experience – at Mercer University – Hester admitted she wasn't ready. She didn't get it.

According to Hester, the failure to land her dream job "sent me on a mission to prepare myself the best I could, so if the job ever did come open again I would be the most prepared person for it." In 2001 she became the first woman's golf coach at Nevada-Las Vegas. In 2002, she was named head coach at Arkansas and turned the struggling program around.

Always, though, Hester wanted to return to Athens. "I teed it up for the first time as a Bulldog in 1992, and I think I knew then I wanted to be a coach and ultimately coach here," she said.

The preparation and patience paid off. Her dream job opened

up again, and she was ready this time. In June 2007, Kelley Hester was named the fourth head coach of the UGA women's golf team.

It took a while, but Kelley Hester's dream came true.

You have dreams. Maybe to make a lot of money. Write the great American novel. Or have the fairy-tale romance.

But dreams often are crushed beneath the weight of everyday living; reality, not dreams, comes to occupy your time, attention, and effort. You've come to understand that achieving your dreams requires a combination of persistence, timing, and providence.

But what if your dreams don't come true because they're not good enough? That is, they're based on the rather alluring but totally unreliable promises of the world rather than the true promises of God, which are a sure thing.

God calls us to great achievements because God's dreams for us are greater than our dreams for ourselves. Such greatness occurs, though, only when our dreams and God's will for our lives are the same.

Your dreams should be worthy of your best – and worthy of God's involvement in making them come true.

An athlete cannot run with money in his pocket. He must run with hope in his heart and dreams in his head.

-- Olympic Gold Medalist Emil Zatopek

Dreams based on the world's promises are often crushed; those based on God's promises are a sure thing.

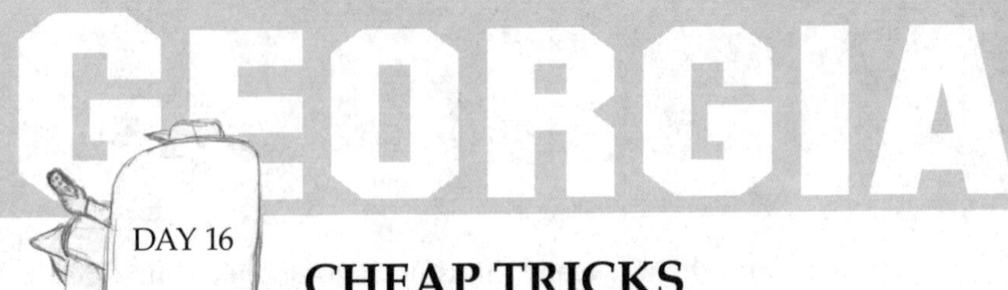

CHEAP TRICKS

Read Acts 19:11-20.

"The evil spirit answered them, 'Jesus I know, and I know about Paul, but who are you?'" (v. 15)

The most famous trick play in Georgia football history never worked — except once.

Alabama came into Sanford Stadium in the 1965 season opener as the defending national champions. Vince Dooley's second team took an early 10-0 lead when tackle Jiggy Smaha forced a fumble and All-American tackle George Patton grabbed the ball and went 55 yards for a touchdown.

Alabama rallied to lead 17-10, though, as the clock wound down to two minutes left to play.

Sitting at their own 27, the Dogs needed what Dooley called a "desperation play," and they had one ready – or sort of. Dooley called for the flea flicker.

Quarterback Kirby Moore's response when the call came in? "C'mon, [Coach Dooley] didn't call that. Tell me the play." When he was convinced, Moore said to the team, "All right, guys. Remember that thing we ran that never worked in practice? We're going to run it. Flea flicker!"

Running back Bob Taylor couldn't believe the call either. When the play was installed in practice, he "thought it was a joke. It looked like something that you would run in grade school. . . . And it never, ever worked in practice. So I never thought we would run it in a game!"

The trick play that never worked was executed perfectly. End Pat Hodgson ran a curl, and Moore hit him with the pass. Hodgson lateraled to a trailing Taylor, who went 73 yards for the miracle touchdown. Moore then hit Hodgson for the two-point conversion on a play the team had executed repeatedly in practice for the legendary 18-17 win.

Scam artists are everywhere — and they love trick plays. An e-mail encourages you to send money to some foreign country to get rich. That guy at your front door offers to resurface your driveway at a ridiculously low price. A TV ad promises a pill to help you lose weight without diet or exercise.

You've been around; you check things out before deciding. The same approach is necessary with spiritual matters, too, because false religions and bogus Christian denominations abound. The key is what any group does with Jesus. Is he the son of God, the ruler of the universe, and the only way to salvation? If not, then what the group espouses is something other than the true Word of God.

The good news about Jesus does indeed sound too good to be true. But the only catch is that there is no catch. No trick -- just the truth.

When you run trick plays and they work, you're a genius. But when they don't work, folks question your sanity.

-- Bobby Bowden

God's promises through Jesus sound too good to be true, but the only catch is that there is no catch.

THE PURLOINED PIG

Read Genesis 9:1-7.

"Everything that lives and moves will be food for you. Just as I gave you the green plants, I now give you everything" (v. 3).

The drive to the 1980 national championship may well have started with a stolen pig.

The football players didn't have any money to buy food for their traditional party after spring practice, and All-American cornerback Scott Woerner suggested they steal a pig from the university hog farm. Five seniors pulled the caper: Woerner, rover Chris Welton, linebacker Frank Ros, and offensive linemen Nat Hudson and Hugh Nall. Nall was recruited because he was an avid outdoorsman with a bow and arrow; Hudson had some experience with barbecuing hogs.

The party was a great success, and the seniors might have gotten away with it except that some freshmen players dumped the hog's head at the feet of a kissing couple. The girl screamed; the guy got a license plate number. The jig – or the pig – was up. Coach Vince Dooley revoked the seniors' scholarships and sentenced them to spend the summer painting the wall around the practice field during the heat of the day.

Why would that be the impetus for a national championship drive? The incident became a catalyst for unprecedented team unity. The five seniors drew closer that summer, and the younger guys were impressed with the way they accepted responsibility. "The five of us, we were the team leaders," Woerner recalled. "It brought a lot of people together." Ros said everybody on the team offered to help: "To a man, they all came to my room and offered to chip in to pay for the pig." Ros said Coach Erk Russell told him he was glad the whole thing happened.

Belly up to the buffet, boys and girls, for barbecue, sirloin steak, grilled chicken, and fried catfish with hush puppies. Rachael Ray's a household name; hamburger joints, pizza parlors, and taco stands lurk on every corner; and we have a TV channel devoted exclusively to food. We love our chow.

Food is one of God's really good ideas, but consider the complex divine plan that gets that pork chop into your mouth. The creator of all life devised a system in which living things are sustained and nourished physically through the sacrifice of other living things in a way similar to what Christ underwent to save you spiritually. Whether it's fast food or home-cooked, everything you eat is a gift from God secured through a divine plan in which some plants and animals have given up their lives.

Pausing to give thanks before you dive in seems the least you can do.

We had some good people, and the attitude was good, but I believe we built on the hog story.

-- Erk Russell on the 1980 national champions

God created a system that nourishes you through the sacrifice of other living things; that's worth a thank-you.

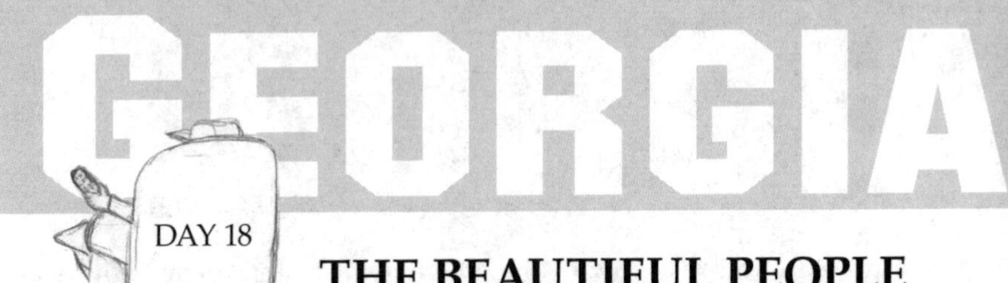

DAY 18

THE BEAUTIFUL PEOPLE

Read Matthew 23:23-28.

> *"Woe to you, teachers of the law and Pharisees, you hypocrites! You are like whitewashed tombs, which look beautiful on the outside, but on the inside are full of dead men's bones and everything unclean" (v. 27).*

Six feet tall. Blond. In *Glamour* magazine.

And she was a self-professed gym rat who was one of Georgia's greatest volleyball players ever.

Though she scoffed at the notion, Nikki Nicholson was amused and intrigued by the idea of being a cover girl. "If somebody's stupid enough to pay me for how I look, I'll do it," she once said.

Nicholson played volleyball for UGA from 1992-95. She was All-SEC all four years, second team All-America twice, and All-South Region three times. She is third all-time in the Georgia record book for kills and attacks and fifth in hitting percentage.

In 1995, *Glamour* magazine named her one of the Top Ten College Women of America. She was described as "beautifully wide-eyed" about the whole business, asserting, "All I do is play volleyball." Not quite. In addition to her looks and her athletic ability, Nicholson was a dedicated student fascinated by – of all things – germs. "I love pathogens," she said of the microorganisms that cause disease. What she means is "she loves the idea of chasing them down and understanding them."

Nicholson called herself a gym rat because even as a 5-year-old, she was at the gym playing ball of some kind.

She was a luminescent volleyball star and a microbiology major who did research at Georgia on a strain of bacteria that infects pigs and birds and whose declared aim in life is "to help people. . . . I'm old-fashioned enough to want to make a difference."

Nikki Nicholson is one of the beautiful people.

Remember the brunette who sat behind you in history class? Or the blonde in English? And how about that hunk from the next apartment who washes his car every Saturday morning and just forces you to get outside earlier than you really want to?

We do love those beautiful people.

It is worth remembering amid our adulation of superficial beauty that *Vogue* or *People* probably wouldn't have been too enamored of Jesus' looks. Isaiah 53 declares that our savior "had no beauty or majesty to attract us to him, nothing in his appearance that we should desire him."

Though Jesus never urged folks to walk around with body odor and unwashed hair, he did admonish us to avoid being overly concerned with physical beauty, which fades with age despite tucks and Botox. What matters to God is inner beauty, which reveals itself in the practice of justice, mercy, and faith, and which is not only lifelong but eternal.

Ah, the glories of women's sports: the camaraderie. The quiet dignity. The proud refusal to buy into traditional stereotypes of beauty.

-- Sports Illustrated for Women

When it comes to looking good to God, it's what's inside that counts.

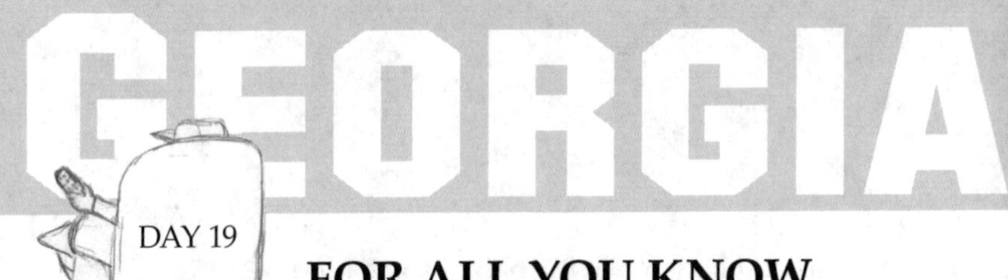

FOR ALL YOU KNOW

Read John 8:12-32.

"You will know the truth, and the truth will set you free" (v. 32).

Maybe there's some truth to the old adage that what you don't know won't hurt you. In Durward Pennington's case, ignorance served him well in the most important kick of his college life.

The Dogs had been picked by the experts to finish ninth or tenth in the SEC in 1959, but when they opened the season by whipping Alabama 17-3, they raised a few eyebrows – and kept raising them. Wins over Vanderbilt, Mississippi State, Kentucky, and Florida set up a mammoth clash with Auburn with the SEC championship on the line.

Many fans with good memories still consider this the most exciting game ever played in Sanford Stadium, considering how important it was. On fourth and 13 with 30 seconds left in the game, Fran Tarkenton hit end Bill Herron with a touchdown pass to tie the game 13-13. Tarkenton called it "the biggest touchdown pass I ever threw."

But that only tied the game; the crucial extra point remained. Tarkenton said, "We were really nervous as Durward Pennington came in to kick the point. He was so calm I couldn't believe it."

Pennington's kick was true, and players and fans alike went berserk. Tarkenton later asked Pennington how he could be so calm and collected. "Somehow during all that excitement he got confused," Tarkenton said. "He thought we were leading 13-12 after the touchdown; that the winning point did not matter."

What Pennington didn't know in this case actually helped him. His kick propelled Georgia to the SEC championship and into the Orange Bowl, a 14-0 win over Missouri.

Unlike Durward Pennington, you may know the score, but there's still much you just flat don't know. Maybe it's the formula for the area of a cylinder or the capital of Myanmar. You may not know how paper is made from trees. Or how toothpaste gets into the tube. And can you honestly say you know how the opposite sex thinks?

Despite your ignorance about certain subjects, you manage quite well because what you don't know generally doesn't hurt you too much. In certain aspects of your life, though, ignorance is anything but harmless. Imagine, for instance, the consequence of not knowing how to do your job. Or of getting behind the wheel without knowing how to drive a car.

And in your faith life, what you don't know can have awful, eternal consequences. To willfully choose not to know Jesus is to be condemned to an eternity apart from God. When it comes to Jesus, knowing the truth sets you free; ignoring the truth enslaves you.

It's what you learn after you know it all that counts.

– John Wooden

What you don't know may not hurt you except when it comes to Jesus.

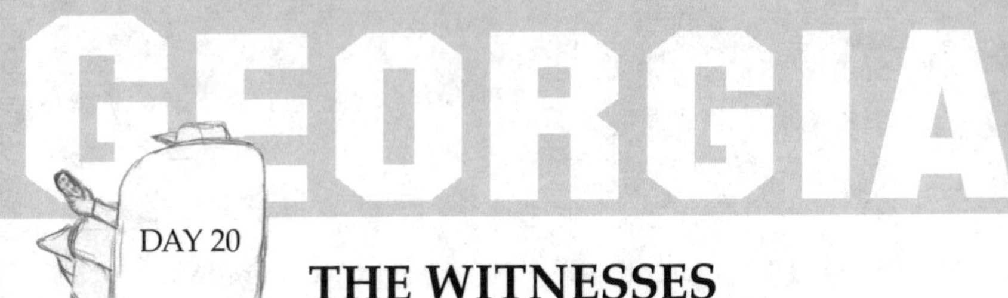

THE WITNESSES

Read Hebrews 11:39-12:2.

"Therefore, since we are surrounded by such a great cloud of witnesses, . . . let us run with perseverance the race marked out for us" (v. 12:1).

They were the witnesses to athletic history at UGA, 1,355 of them.

They were the "sunburned fans scattered on the hillsides surrounding the fenced field" on which was played the first-ever UGA intercollegiate soccer game. On Sept. 3, 1995, women's soccer began at Georgia with a 4-0 win over Georgia State.

Twenty-two players, 21 of them freshmen, made up the historic squad that launched the first new varsity sport at UGA in 16 years. Mandy Aiken, who played at the Lovett School, said of the new team, "We don't know what to expect. But everyone is real good, so you have to be motivated or someone may pass you by." "We're all a little bit nervous," said defender Kristin Jacobsen, who played on two state championship teams at McIntosh High School in Fayette County. "But it's great to be part of something new."

They began the program with a win. Danya Harris from Sanford, Fla., scored the program's first-ever goal eight minutes into the game.

And those 1,355 witnesses to history? They don't seem like a very big crowd considering how many pack Sanford Stadium on a Saturday afternoon in September. But for the new Georgia soccer players the crowd was just fine, bigger than expected in fact. "It's the best thing I've ever experienced in soccer," Harris said. "I've never played in a game with that many people watching before."

Still, the crowd was a reminder that even at UGA many athletes play outside the packed arenas and away from the TV cameras.

You, too, probably don't have a huge crowd of folks applauding your efforts every day, and you certainly don't have TV cameras broadcasting your every move to an enthralled audience. Sometimes you may even feel alone. A child's illness, the slow death of a loved one, financial troubles, worries about your health – you feel isolated.

But a person of faith is never alone, and not just because you're aware of God's presence. You are always surrounded by a crowd of God's most faithful witnesses, those in the present and those from the past. Their faithfulness both encourages and inspires. They, too, have faced the difficult circumstances with which you contend, and they remained faithful and true to God.

With their examples before you, you can endure your trials, looking in hope and faithfulness beyond your immediate troubles to God's glorious future. Your final victory in Christ will be even sweeter because of your struggles.

A very small crowd here today. I can count the people on one hand. Can't be more than 30.

– Announcer Michael Abrahamson

The person of faith is surrounded by a crowd of witnesses whose faithfulness in difficult times inspires us to remain true to God no matter what.

CHANGELESS

Read Hebrews 13:4-16.

"Jesus Christ is the same yesterday and today and forever" (v. 8).

What game is this?

Players letting their hair grow long for protection because they didn't wear helmets. Spectators rushing onto the field and getting in the players' way. A watermelon-shaped ball, too big to hold in your hand and pass. Games called on account of darkness.

A nose guard was about the only protection a player had. Maybe shoulder pads and hip pads, but only if he provided them himself.

Scrambling to find an opponent to play because no one scheduled any games. A slanted field rather than a level one. A player hiding the ball under a jersey. No scoreboard. A player kicking a field goal by setting the ball on his helmet. The length of the halves to be determined by agreement of the teams and usually depending upon the weather. Teammates dragging a tackled ball carrier forward. A Georgia player dressed in civilian clothes hiding in the crowd until the play begins and then catching a pass.

What game is this?

This was the wild, wacky, and wooly game of college football in its early days, the 1890s and the turn of the century. Largely unregulated and unsophisticated with no forward pass, it was a game we would barely recognize today.

Thank goodness, we might well say. Given the symmetry, the excitement, the passion, and the sheer spectacle that surround today's college game, few, if any, Georgia Bulldog fans would long for the days when handles were sewn into the pants of ball carriers to make them easier to toss.

Like everything else, football has changed. Computers and CDs, cell phones and George Foreman grills, iPods and IMAX theaters – they and much that is in your life now may not have even been around when you were 16. Think about how style, cars, communications, and tax laws constantly change.

Don't be too harsh on the world, though, because you've changed also. You've aged, gained or lost weight, gotten married, changed jobs, or relocated.

Have you ever found yourself bewildered by the rapid pace of change, casting about for something to hold on to that will always be the same, that you can use as an anchor for your life? Is there anything like that?

Sadly, the answer's no. All the things of this world change.

On the other hand, there's Jesus, who is the same today, the same forever, always dependable, always loving you. No matter what happens in your life, Jesus is still the same.

I believe in the power of sport and play to change lives.
-- Olympic Gold Medalist Catriona Le May Doan

In our ever-changing and bewildering world, Jesus is the same forever; his love for you will never change.

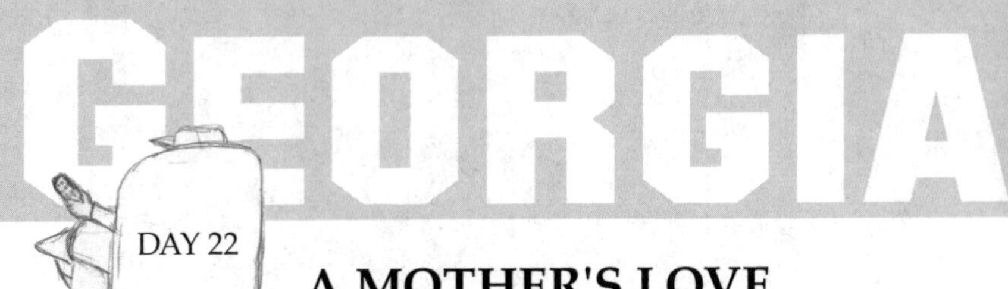

A MOTHER'S LOVE

Read John 19:25-30.

"Near the cross of Jesus stood his mother" (v. 25).

"Thank goodness for Elaine Bailey."

Bulldog fans can certainly shout a vociferous "Amen" to that! Elaine Bailey is the matriarch of the Bailey family of Folkston, which has produced the "most acclaimed, illustrious, and just plain great set of brothers in Georgia football history."

The senior Bailey brother, Ronald, set the precedent when he came to Athens in 1993 and had a fine career as a defensive back from 1995-97.

Next came Roland, better known as "Champ," "the most versatile player at Georgia since the inception of two-platoon football" in the 1950s. A 1998 All-America, Champ played wide receiver on offense, cornerback on defense, and returned punts and kickoffs on special teams. Seven times during the 1998 season, he was in on more than 100 plays. Coach Jim Donnan once called Champ a "dinosaur," a throwback to the days when players excelled on both sides of the ball. "He can do whatever you need him to do on the football field," Donnan said.

Rodney "Boss" Bailey followed his older brothers to Athens in 1998. Also an All-America, Boss was a captain for the 2002 SEC champions, leading the team in tackles and getting six quarterback sacks.

God blessed the Bailey brothers with ability and size, but their good fortune in life is the result of more than God-given talent. Boss once said they owe much that has been good about their lives to their mother, Elaine. "She's the center of everything," Boss said. "Everything goes through her. It never stops with my mom."

That's the way it often is with mamas. They are the center of their children's lives, even going so far as sacrificing personal happiness for the sake of their sons and daughters.

No mother in history, though, has faced a challenge to match that of Mary, whom God chose to be the mother of Jesus. Like mamas and their children throughout time, Mary experienced both joy and perplexity in her relationship with her son.

To the end, though, Mary stood by her boy. She followed him all the way to his execution, an act of love and bravery since Jesus was condemned as an enemy of the Roman Empire.

But just as mothers like Elaine Bailey and Mary – and perhaps yours -- would apparently do anything for their children, so will God do anything out of love for his children. After all, that was God on the cross at the foot of which Mary stood, and he was dying for you, one of his children.

Everyone should find time to write and to go see their mother. I think that's healthy.

– Bear Bryant

Mamas often sacrifice for their children, but God, too, will do anything out of love for his children, including dying on a cross.

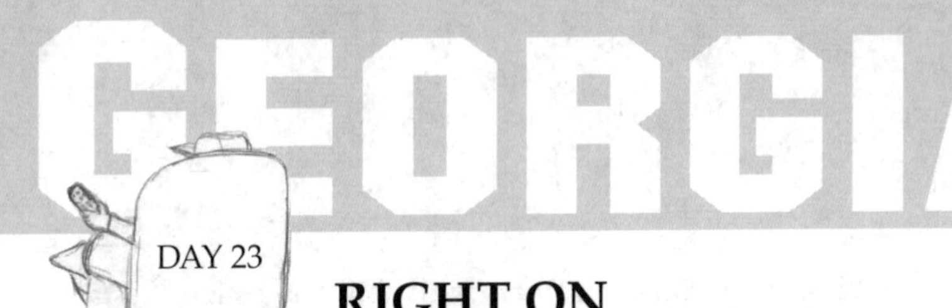

RIGHT ON

Read Galatians 6:7-10.

"Let us not grow weary in doing what is right, for we will reap at harvest time, if we do not give up" (v. 9 NRSV).

Kim Thompson was so nervous about her first high-school basketball game that she almost didn't leave the locker room. But her anxiety wasn't about the game; it was about her uniform.

Though she stood only 5-feet-5, Thompson was just the fifth freshmen in UGA history to start her first collegiate game. (The others were Adrienne Shuler, Tammye Jenkins, Lady Hardmon, and Camille Lowe.) She lettered all four years from 1993-96 and was part of the 1996 SEC champions and national runners-up. And she played all that ball in the same kind of uniform that caused her so much anxiety back in high school.

Kim Thompson played basketball in a skirt. She wore it because her Pentecostal faith enforced a dress code prohibiting women from wearing pants (Deuteronomy 22:5).

"I was so scared," Thompson said about that first game. "Everyone else had been out on the floor, warmed up, come back into the locker room and went back out on the floor. I was sitting in the locker room in my skirt the whole time. The coach had to drag me out."

He did, and she played, scoring 32 points.

Thompson's basketball career had her family's support with a key provision. "We have a standard with the Lord to keep," her mother explained. Kim Thompson kept it. "I don't let it affect my game," she said. "If the players want to stand there and look at my skirt, then that's fine with me because I'm going to dribble right past them."

Kim Thompson did the right thing even if it set her apart from the crowd and set her up for some ridicule.

Doing the right thing is easy when it's little stuff. Giving the quarter back when the cashier gives you too much change, helping a lost child at the mall, or putting a few bucks in the honor box at your favorite fishing hole.

But what about when doing the right thing may well cost you, whether it be financially or emotionally? Every day you have multiple chances to do the right thing; in every instance, you have a choice: right or wrong. The factors that weigh into your decisions – including the personal cost to you – reveal much about your character.

Does your doing the right thing ever depend upon your calculation of the odds of getting caught? In the world's eyes, you can't go wrong doing wrong when you won't get caught. That passes for the world's slippery, situational ethics, but it doesn't pass muster with God.

In God's eyes, you can't go wrong doing right. Ever.

Never compromise what you think is right.

-- Bear Bryant

As far as God is concerned, you can never go wrong doing right.

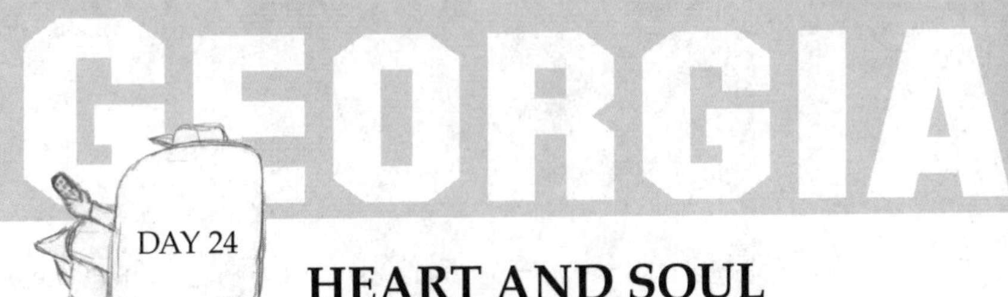

DAY 24

HEART AND SOUL

Read Romans 12:1-2.

"Therefore, I urge you, brothers, in view of God's mercy, to offer your bodies as living sacrifices, holy and pleasing to God – this is your spiritual act of worship" (v. 1).

When Billy Henderson arrived in Athens in 1946 to play football for Georgia, he knew there was no turning back.

But that didn't keep him from having some second thoughts. He rode to Athens from Macon on a bus and walked with a buddy to Milledge Annex, where the football players lived. Henderson recalled that when he walked in, "Weyman Sellers . . . was doing pushups, and somebody was counting for him. When that guy started counting '85, 86, 87' I turned to my buddy and said, 'I think we better go back home.'"

Henderson realized quickly that things were going to be very different now. Each year head coach Wally Butts picked a particular freshman who would serve as the example to everyone else for just how things were going to be. In 1946, Henderson was Coach Butts' freshman. Once when Butts was talking to him, Henderson reached down to tie his shoe, and Butts knocked him down. The coach, Henderson said, insisted that his players look him in the eye when he was talking to them and "if you were not paying full attention to him, he would let you know it."

Still, he couldn't turn back. "My daddy died when I was eight years old, and my mother had four kids to raise," Henderson remembered. "I pretty much knew that when I got to Georgia that would be it. There would be no going back. I was on my own."

Billy Henderson, who would become one of the state's most successful high-school coaches and whose son, Johnny, would play on the 1976 SEC champions, was committed.

When you stood in a church and recited your wedding vows, did you make a decision that you could walk away from when things got tough or did you make a lifelong commitment? Is your job just a way to get a paycheck, or are you committed to it?

Commitment seems almost a dirty word in our society these days, a synonym for chains, an antonym for freedom. Perhaps this is why so many people are afraid of Jesus: Jesus demands commitment. To speak of offering yourself as "a living sacrifice" is not to speak blithely of making a decision but of heart-body-mind-and-soul commitment.

But commitment actually means "purpose and meaning," especially when you're talking about your life. Commitment makes life worthwhile. Anyway, in insisting upon commitment, Jesus isn't asking anything from you that he hasn't already given to you himself. His commitment to you was so deep that he died for you.

There are only two options regarding commitment. You're either in or you're out. There is no such thing as life in-between.

-- Pat Riley

Rather than constraining you,
commitment to Jesus lends meaning to your life,
releasing you to move forward with purpose.

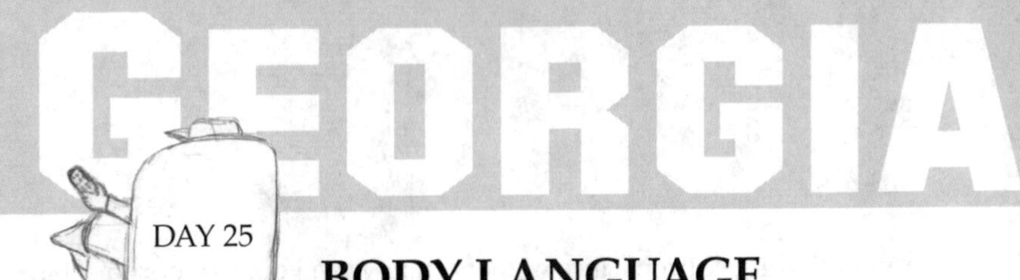

DAY 25

BODY LANGUAGE

Read 1 Corinthians 6:12-20.

"Do you not know that your body is a temple of the Holy Spirit, who is in you, whom you have received from God? . . . Honor God with your body" (vv. 19, 20b).

It's hard to believe now, but in the early days, Georgia's football facilities were pretty pitiful.

In 1965, tackle Hugh Gordon, who played for Georgia at the turn of the century, remembered the lack of training facilities and other amenities. "We would have been run off the field by any freshman team of today," he said. "We knew nothing of conditioning, had no training table, and ate anywhere and anything we pleased."

"We wore the same uniform for practice as in the games and toward the end of the season we were a disreputable sight. No two uniforms looked alike," Gordon recalled.

His assertion that the players were in lousy shape is borne out by a report of the 1900 game against Tech, which Georgia won 12-0: "On account of the poor physical condition of the men, the halves were cut to fifteen minutes each." The report groused that had the game been allowed its full thirty minutes, "the Techs would have scored since the Georgia boys were badly in need of wind."

The players weren't the only thing in need of some work. They had only an "old dressing room in the basement of Old

College." Professor Charles Herty, the "Father of Georgia Football," complained to alums after the 1896 season that the university's football field, which would later bear his name, was an "old red dirt field." Another description called the site, "a playing field of sorts, bare and stubbly." Herty said the teams won in spite of what he called "the poorest equipment . . . in the South."

You may feel a little bit like an "old red dirt field" when you look into a mirror and critically examine your personal playing field. Too heavy, too short, too pale, too gray, and where'd all the hair go? We often compare ourselves to an impossible standard Hollywood and fashion magazines have created, and we are inevitably disappointed.

God must have been quite partial to your body, though, because he personally fashioned it and gave it to you free of charge. Your body, like everything else in your life, is thus a gift from God.

But God didn't stop there. He then quite voluntarily chose to inhabit your body, sharing it with you in the person of the Holy Spirit.

What an act of consummate ungratefulness it is then to abuse your God-given body by violating God's standards for living. To do so is in fact to dishonor God.

If you don't do what's best for your body, you're the one who comes up on the short end.

-- Julius Erving

You may not have a fine opinion of your body, but God thought enough of it to personally create it for you.

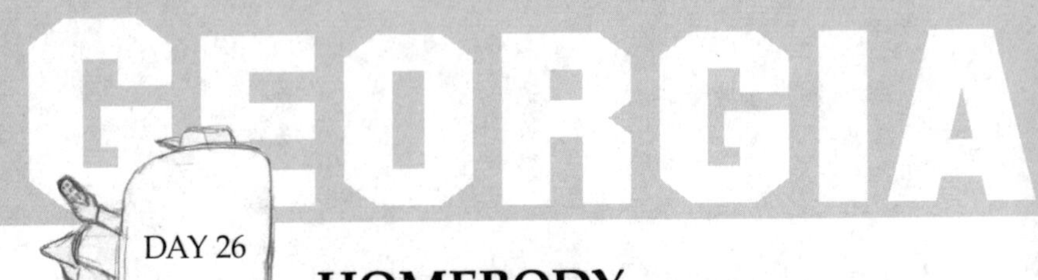

HOMEBODY

Read 2 Corinthians 5:1-10.

"We . . . would prefer to be away from the body and at home with the Lord" (v. 8).

Gudrun Arnardottir was a long, long, long way from home, and she was homesick.

The Georgia track and field athlete with the most perfect first name ever for her sport – it's pronounced "good run" – was a leading member of Coach John Mitchell's 1995 SEC outdoor champions (Georgia's first) and the 1996 indoor SEC runners-up. Arnardottir was an SEC champion six times from 1994-96 and was on the SEC Academic Honor Roll in 1995 and 1996. She still holds the school records for the 400-meter dash, the 55-meter hurdles, the 100-meter hurdles, and the 400-meter hurdles.

But when she arrived in Athens, she was just like most college freshman; she was in a strange place and she was homesick. Only for her, Athens was stranger than for most other freshmen. That's because Arnardottir hailed from Iceland, and the strangeness only intensified her homesickness. "I felt isolated," she said. "You don't know where anything is, where the store is, how to get there. I hate that. But then I realized all the freshmen here, they are lost, too."

It didn't hurt that her teammates on the track team hailed from all over the world: Finland, Scotland, Jamaica, the Bahamas, Canada, and the United States of Georgia (Elberton, Waynesboro, and Atlanta). "We find it pretty cool," she said about the little United Nations that was the Georgia team. "It's kind of a funny mixture. . . . What we all have in common is the track."

Once she settled in a bit, Arnardottir grew to love Athens, the friendliness of the Southerners around her, and their open and deep faith. The Classic City came to feel like home.

As Gudrun Arnardottir learned, home is not necessarily a matter of geography. It may be that place you share with your spouse and your children, whether it's Georgia or Iceland. You may feel at home when you return to Athens, wondering why you were so eager to leave in the first place. Maybe the home you grew up in still feels like an old shoe, a little worn but comfortable and inviting.

God planted that sense of home in us because he is a God of place, and our place is with him. Thus, we may live a few blocks away from our parents and grandparents or we may relocate every few years, but we still will sometimes feel as though we don't really belong no matter where we are.

We don't; our true home is with God in the place Jesus has gone ahead to prepare for us. We are homebodies and we are perpetually homesick.

Everybody's better at home.

-- Basketball player Justin Dentmon

We are continually homesick for our real home, which is with God in Heaven.

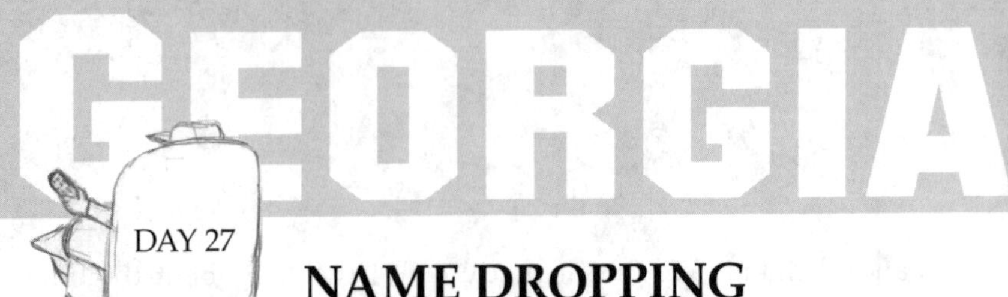

NAME DROPPING

Read Exodus 3:1-15.

"This is my name forever, the name by which I am to be remembered from generation to generation" (v. 15).

Deanna "Tweety" Nolan. Goat Jernigan. Spec Towns.

They just keep coming: nicknames and appellations slapped onto Georgia's often colorful and legendary athletes and coaches.

Rufus "Cow" Nalley invented the huddle in 1895. Pop Warner was Georgia's first full-time paid coach. Bobby Walden was "The Big Toe from Cairo," Herschel Walker was "The Goal Line Stalker," and Dominique Wilkins was "The Human Highlight Film." All-American tackle Mike "Moonpie" Wilson blocked beside Joel "Cowboy" Parrish. Remember Coach J.B. "Ears" Whitworth and Zippy Morocco? George "Kid" Woodruff coached Georgia from 1923-1927 for a dollar a year. The 1932 Southern Conference basketball champions included Catfish Smith, Flip Costa, and Big Bill Strickland.

Don't forget Zeke Bratkowski, Glidin' Glynn Harrison, Eddie "Meat Cleaver" Weaver, and Champ and Boss Bailey (Roland and Rodney). In perhaps the greatest moniker of all, Dan Magill dubbed German-born kicker Peter Rajecki "The Bootin' Teuton." Magill also came up with what might be the strangest nickname in Georgia history when he labeled fullback Ronnie Jenkins "The Ebullient Embalmer" for his tendency to smile after he bulldozed over would-be tacklers.

BULLDOGS

Bramwell W. "Bump" Gabrielsen was such an excellent swim coach in the 1950s he won the SEC championship without any scholarshipped swimmers. Harold "War Eagle" Ketron played for Georgia at the turn of the century and once punched out the opposing head coach because he was yelling instructions to his players and the officials wouldn't stop him. (See Devotion #83.)

Nicknames associated with Bulldogs players and coaches are not slapped haphazardly upon individuals but rather reflect widely held perceptions about the person named. Proper names do that also.

Nowhere throughout history has this concept been more prevalent that in the Bible, where a name is not a mere label but is an expression of the essential nature of the named one. That is, a person's name reveals his or her character. Even God shares this concept; to know the name of God is to know God as he has chosen to reveal himself to us.

What does your name say about you? Honest, trustworthy, a seeker of the truth and a person of God? Or does the mention of your name cause your coworkers to whisper snide remarks, your neighbors to roll their eyes, or your friends to start making allowances for you?

Most importantly, what does your name say about you to God? He, too, knows you by name.

There are sports names, and then there are sports names. Buck Belue. I've heard few better.

-- Loran Smith

Live so that your name evokes positive associations by people you know, the public, and God.

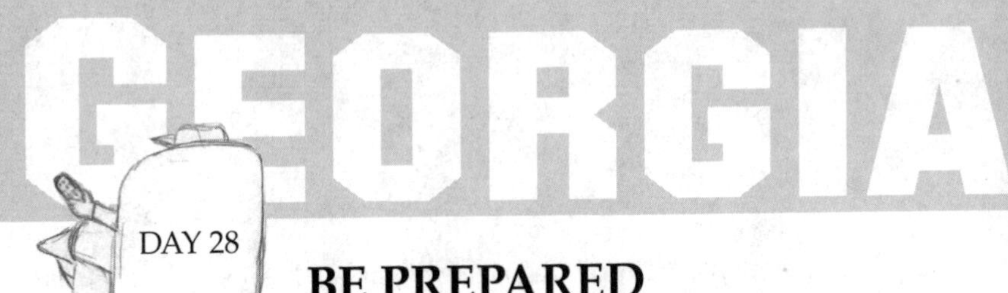

BE PREPARED

Read Matthew 10:5-23.

"I am sending you out like sheep among wolves. Therefore be as shrewd as snakes and as innocent as doves" (v. 16).

The play called for the quarterback to run a sweep – with nobody blocking for him.

That quarterback was Ray Goff, who was the captain of Georgia's 1976 SEC champions and the SEC Player of the Year. He served as Georgia's head football coach from 1989 through 1995.

When those strange instructions calling for no blocking were given, Goff's reaction was understandable. "I really didn't like that idea at all," he said. But in the 1975 game against Vanderbilt with Georgia struggling with a 7-3 lead, the play had a purpose. Offensive line coach Jimmy Vickers had noticed on film that on defense Vanderbilt always huddled right next to the ball and held hands, so he came up with a play to take advantage of that.

Goff was supposed to run the sweep but get tackled before he went out of bounds. He said, "I did my job and ran the sweep with no blocking and, of course, they killed me." The ref then spotted the ball on the near hash mark, and Vandy huddled up, holding hands. Goff walked over to the ball and knelt down as though he were tying a shoe. The rest of the team was across the field. With the Commodores still holding hands, Goff shoveled the ball over to Gene Washington, who had a convoy to the goal line. Nobody ever touched him. The play broke open a tight game, and Georgia won 47-3.

The shoestring play, as it was called, worked because the Dog coaches had prepared the team and the preceding play had prepared Vanderbilt.

Just like the Dogs with their game plan, you know the importance of preparation in your own life. You went to the bank for a car loan, facts and figures in hand. That presentation you made at work was seamless because you practiced. The kids' school play suffered no meltdowns because they rehearsed. Knowing what you need to do and doing what you must to succeed isn't luck; it's preparation.

Jesus understood this, and he prepared his followers by lecturing them and by sending them on field trips. Two thousand years later, the life of faith requires similar training and study. You prepare so you'll be ready when that unsaved neighbor standing beside you at your backyard grill asks about Jesus. You prepare so you will know how God wants you to live. You prepare so you are certain in what you believe when the secular, godless world challenges it.

And one day you'll see God face to face. You certainly want to be prepared for that.

Spectacular achievements are always preceded by unspectacular preparation.

-- Roger Staubach

Living in faith requires constant study and training, preparation for the day when you meet God face to face.

A DOG'S LIFE

Read Genesis 6:11-22; 8:1-4.

"God remembered Noah and all the wild animals and the livestock that were with him in the ark" (v. 8:1).

Short of Rin Tin Tin and Lassie, he may well be the most well known and best publicized dog in the country.

After all, he has appeared in two movies and been featured on the cover of *Sports Illustrated*, which declared him the best college mascot in the country. He was the first mascot to be invited to the Downtown Athletic Club for the presentation of the Heisman Trophy. He dressed for the occasion with his own tuxedo.

He is, of course, Uga.

In the 1920s, Georgia's football team acquired the nickname "Bulldogs" when a sportswriter described their play as "tenacious as a Bulldog." Over the years, various families loaned their bulldogs for certain games.

From 1947 to 1955, the university mascot was two brindled English bulldogs, Butch (1947-50) and Mike (1951-55). When Mike died, Coach Wally Butts asked Dan Magill, the sports information director, to find a replacement.

Replying to a story Magill had placed in area newspapers, a Georgia law student named Sonny Seiler told Magill his wife and he had a puppy that just might work. He was the grandson of the mascot who had made the trip to the 1943 Rose Bowl. Magill went by the young couple's apartment, saw the puppy, and told Butts the dog looked good. "Put him to work," Butts said.

The rest, so to speak, is Bulldog history.

Today, Uga VII presides over the gathering of the Bulldog faithful, enjoying victories at Sanford Stadium from the comfort of his air-conditioned dog house. It's a dog life indeed.

Do you have a dog or two around the place? How about a cat that passes time staring longingly at your caged canary? Kids have gerbils? Maybe you've gone more exotic with a tarantula or a ferret.

Americans love our pets; in fact, more households in this country have pets than have children. We not only share our living space with animals we love and protect but also with some – such as roaches and rats – that we seek to exterminate.

None of us, though, has the problems Noah faced when he packed God's menagerie into one boat. God saved all his varmints from extinction, including the fish and the ducks, who were probably quite delighted with the whole flood business.

The lesson is clear for we who strive to live as God wants us to: All living things are under God's care. It isn't just our cherished pets that God calls us to care for and respect; we are to serve God as stewards of all of his creatures.

Uga is the best mascot a team could have. He'll lay on you. He'll lick on you. Give him a bone and he'll love you for life.

-- Former Bulldog end Clarence Kay

God cares about all his creatures, and he expects us to respect them too.

HOME IMPROVEMENT

Read Ephesians 4:7-16.

"The body of Christ may be built up until we all reach unity in the faith and in the knowledge of the Son of God and become mature, attaining to the whole measure of the fullness of Christ" (vv. 12b, 13).

She once admitted she "couldn't run down the court without falling down about every three steps." Coach Andy Landers said that at practice the other Lady Dogs "just chewed her up and spit her out every day."

It's not that Mary Beth Lycett was someone who happened to wander into Lady Dog basketball practice one afternoon. She came to Athens in 1999 as Miss Georgia Basketball, but she "played more like Miss Manners." It didn't help that she found herself a freshman on a team with four future professional players: Kelly and Coco Miller, Deanna "Tweety" Nolan, and Kiesha Brown. "None of them was much bothered by the new kid. I couldn't guard anybody," Lycett admitted. "It was rough." It was so rough that one writer called each practice "another voyage of humiliation" for Lycett.

"I had to get better or get killed every day," Lycett said. So she worked hard, ran harder, and got better. Her extra runs were legendary among the athletic offices. Athletic Director Vince Dooley, in fact, routinely greeted Landers with "saw Mary Beth out running this morning."

Before it was over, Landers said Lycett made the greatest improvement of any player he had ever run across in his 29 seasons of coaching. She started 50 of 60 games her last two seasons in Athens and developed into the team's most dependable three-point shooter. She improved so much that one of Landers' biggest questions after the 2002-03 season was how he was going to replace her.

Just as Mary Beth Lycett did, you try to improve at whatever you tackle. You attend training sessions and seminars to do your job better. You take golf or tennis lessons and practice to get better. You play that new video game until you master it. To get better at anything requires a dedication involving practice, training, study, and preparation.

Your faith life is no different. Jesus calls us to improve ourselves spiritually by becoming more mature in our faith. We can always know more about God's word, discover more ways to serve God, deepen our prayer life and our trust in God, and do a better job of being Jesus to other people through simple acts of kindness and caring. In other words, we can always become more like Jesus.

One day we will all stand before God as finished products. We certainly want to present him a mature dwelling, a spiritual mansion, not a hovel.

The principle is competing against yourself. It's about self-improvement, about being better than you were the day before.

-- Former NFL quarterback Steve Young

Spiritual improvement means a constant effort to become more like Jesus in our day-to-day lives.

PLAN AHEAD

Read Psalm 33:1-15.

"The plans of the Lord stand firm forever, the purposes of his heart through all generations" (v. 11).

Coach Mark Richt had a rather unusual plan to get his team playing the way he knew they had to: get penalized or get punished!

When Knowshon Moreno stretched into the end zone for the first score against Florida on Oct. 27, 2007, the Dogs raised excessive celebration to a new level. The entire team – more than 60 players -- ran onto the field and celebrated, drawing a penalty -- just as Richt had planned.

Richt confessed he ordered the first-score celebration two weeks before the game. "I told them," he said, "'when we score our first touchdown, if we don't get a celebration penalty, I'm going to run every one of y'all at 5:45 in the morning.'" Why would he say such a thing? "I wanted the guys to be in a frenzy." Richt knew that his team would be in trouble against Florida if they didn't play with passion, so he ordered the team celebration to create some excitement. Quarterback Matthew Stafford backed up his boss' reasoning. "We had been playing a little dull the last few games," he said, "and we just wanted to get everybody going."

The plan caused the defensive coaches considerable anxiety, which worsened when the Dogs were hit with two penalties for the celebration. They wound up kicking off from the eight yard line. "We were saying, 'Whoa, whoa, whoa,'" said defensive line coach Rodney Garner. "That can't be right. That's got to be the wrong spot." But it wasn't.

Did the plan work?

Well, when the game ended, the Dogs were still passionate, still frenzied, and still celebrating: 42-30 Dawgs.

Just as successful coaching does, successful living takes planning. You go to school to improve your chances for a better paying job. You use blueprints to build your home. You plan for retirement. You map out your vacation to have the best time. You even plan your children -- sometimes.

Your best-laid plans, however, sometimes get wrecked by events and circumstances beyond your control. The economy goes into the tank; a debilitating illness strikes; a hurricane hits. Life is capricious and thus no plans -- not even your best ones -- are foolproof.

But you don't have to go it alone. God has plans for your life that guarantee success as God defines it if you will make him your planning partner. God's plan for your life includes joy, love, peace, kindness, gentleness, and faithfulness, all the elements necessary for truly successful living for today and for all eternity. And God's plan will not fail.

If you don't know where you are going, you will wind up somewhere else.

-- *Yogi Berra*

Your plans help ensure a successful life; God's plans absolutely ensure a successful eternity.

TOUGH COOKIES

Read 2 Corinthians 11:21b-31.

"Besides everything else, I face daily the pressure of my concern for all the churches" (v. 28).

"All those guys from Georgia are always tough."

That's what rookie Len Hauss heard a Washington Redskins coach say one day during practice at the team's training camp in Pennsylvania.

Hauss was a Bulldog center from 1961-63. He played 14 seasons in the NFL, but at his rookie camp, Hauss said, "I was so scared that it was three weeks before I spoke to anybody." As a rookie, he had to prove himself, and he did one day in an encounter against legendary linebacker Sam Huff.

Hauss wound up opposite Huff during one-on-one drills, and Huff promptly knocked the rookie on his backside. But when Huff came up again, Hauss broke line to get another shot at the legend, and he whispered to the quarterback to change the snap count and go on the first sound. Huff had had the advantage earlier of knowing the count.

This time Hauss put Huff on the ground. "Everybody cheered," Hauss said. "A lot of those guys didn't like Sam because he was so good." But how would the legend react to being shown up by the rookie?

Instead of being angry, Huff picked himself up and said, "That's the way, Hauss. There's an old Georgia Bulldog. I never knew a Georgia Bulldog in my career who wouldn't knock you on your backside."

That's when the coach chipped in with his affirmation that all those Bulldog players were tough. "That meant something to me then, and it still means something to me," Hauss said long after he retired. Everybody knows Georgia Bulldogs are tough.

You don't have to be a Georgia football player to be tough. In America today, toughness isn't restricted to physical accomplishments and brute strength. Going to work every morning even when you feel bad, sticking by your rules for your children in a society that ridicules parental authority, making hard decisions about your aging parents' care, often over their objections – you've got to be tough every day just to live honorably, decently, and justly.

Living faithfully requires toughness, too, though in America chances are you won't be imprisoned, stoned, or flogged this week for your faith as Paul was. Still, contemporary society exerts subtle, psychological, daily pressures on you to turn your back on your faith and your values. Popular culture promotes promiscuity, atheism, and gutter language; your children's schools have kicked God out; the corporate culture advocates amorality before the shrine of the almighty dollar.

You have to hang tough to keep the faith.

Winning isn't imperative, but getting tougher in the fourth quarter is.
– Bear Bryant

Life demands more than mere physical toughness; you must be spiritually tough too.

DAY 33

WORM DROWNING

Read Mark 1:14-20.

"'Come, follow me,' Jesus said, 'and I will make you fishers of men'" (v. 17).

Big Jim Whatley once learned a vital lesson: Shooting a big alligator between the eyes doesn't kill it.

"Big Jim" received his nickname the day he was born. He was an all-star tackle for Alabama, playing next to Bear Bryant. He coached baseball, football, and basketball at Georgia. Whatley was the head baseball coach for 25 seasons, winning 334 games through 1975, his last season at the helm. His 1950 basketball Bulldogs upset Adolph Rupp's Kentucky team 71-60. He was such a spectacular athlete that he could kick out light bulbs in the ceiling, which Dan Magill said "scared the daylights out of many an unsuspecting person."

Whatley was an avid fisherman, and his wife and he vacationed for many summers at Sanibel Island in Florida. One time he encountered a 10-foot alligator while he was fishing. He fetched his rifle from his car, pumped two shots between the gator's eyes and then hoisted the supposedly dead reptile into his trunk to show to his wife, who was off collecting sea shells.

Big Jim hollered for her to come see the treasure he had found for her collection and excitedly opened the trunk only to be greeted by a very alive and very angry alligator that had one thing in mind: to get its jaws wrapped around any of Big Jim's appendages. Whatley slammed the trunk and then did a handstand on it to keep it down while the gator completely destroyed the trunk with its tail.

Only later did Whatley learn that shooting an alligator between the eyes doesn't kill it but merely stuns it.

The worst fishing trip you ever had may have included a foul-tempered gator, numbing cold, or a flat tire. The only thing you caught was a cold, and you dragged in late, knowing full well you had to get up early next morning. Still, it was better than a good day at work, wasn't it?

What if somebody in authority looked right at you and told you, "Go Fish"? How quickly would you trip over anybody who got in your way? Well, Jesus did exactly that, commanding his followers to fish for people who are drowning and lost without him.

Jesus issued that command with the utmost seriousness. For the men of his time, fishing was neither for pleasure nor for sport. Rather, it was hard work, a demanding, hardscrabble way to support a family.

Fishing for men and women for Jesus is likewise hard work, but it is such the essence of the Christian mission that a fish has become the symbol for the faith itself.

Some go to church and think about fishing; others go fishing and think about God.

-- Fisherman Tony Blake

Jesus understood the passion people have for fishing and commanded that it become not just a hobby but a way of life.

FRUIT TREES

Read Matthew 7:15-20.

"By their fruit you will recognize them" (v. 20).

Apples and oranges. They generally don't mix – except in UGA football history.

After losing to Clemson 29-0 in the 1903 opener, the Georgia players – led by captain Harold "War Eagle" Ketron -- struck a deal with the Carolina boys. Clemson was to play Georgia Tech the next week, and Georgia promised them anything they wanted for every point they beat Georgia Tech beyond the 29 by which they had beaten Georgia.

The Clemson players wanted some apples, and the deal was struck. As the *Atlanta Journal* rather condescendingly put it, "Eating apples is said to be the crowning dissipation of the Clemson student body. The town itself has not yet been incorporated on the map and such vicious habits as demon rum, ping pong, and other forms of vice common to a large city are unknown."

Clemson mauled Tech 73-0, and the Georgia players paid off with "forty-four bushels of select, rosey apples, booked at $1 per bushel." Rumor had it that the Georgia Tech players didn't appreciate Georgia's part in their humiliation one bit.

Georgia led TCU 40-7 in the 1942 Orange Bowl when guard Harry Kuniansky took a seat on the bench and began his victory celebration, appropriately enough, with some oranges. He filled his helmet with oranges, squeezed the juice out of them, and set about quenching his thirst when line coach J.B. Whitworth bellowed for him to get back into the game. "Accustomed to instant compliance with [his coach's] orders, [Kuniansky] jammed on his helmet without removing the oranges and raced onto the field with juice streaming down his face."

Strawberry shortcake. Apple pie. Ice-cold watermelon. Banana pudding. Straight up, congealed, or served with whipped cream or ice cream, fresh fruit is hard to beat. We even use it symbolically to represent the good things in our lives: A promotion or a raise is the fruit of our good work.

Fruity metaphors and images conjure up thoughts of something sweet and satisfying. Little in life, however, is as rancid as fruit gone bad. That dual image of fruit at its best and its worst is what Jesus had in mind when he spoke of knowing both false prophets and faithful followers by their fruit.

Our lives as disciples of Jesus should yield not just material fruits but spiritual fruits also. Our spiritual fruits are what we leave in our wake: heartbreak, tears, anger, bitterness, and dissension; or peace, love, joy, generosity, and gentleness.

Good or bad – delicious or rotten -- these are the fruits by which we shall be known by those around us – and by God.

On these fields of friendly strife are sown the seeds that on other fields, and other days, will bear the fruits of victory.

-- Gen. Douglas MacArthur on athletic competition

God knows you by your spiritual fruits, not the material ones the world fancies so.

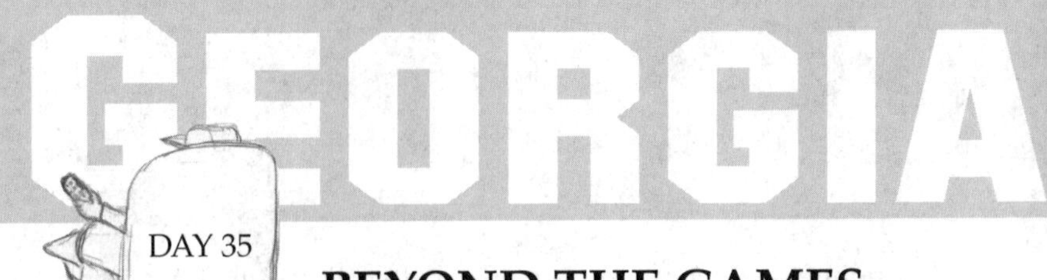

BEYOND THE GAMES

Read Galatians 5:16-26.

"So I say, live by the Spirit. . . . The sinful nature desires what is contrary to the Spirit. . . . The acts of the sinful nature are obvious: . . . I warn you, as I did before, that those who live like this will not inherit the kingdom of God" (vv. 16, 17, 19, 21).

The cold statistics say he wasn't a success at Georgia. Odell Collins knows otherwise.

Collins came to Athens as the next Herschel, the back who would lead Georgia back to championships and big bowl games. Instead, his career statistics showed only 29 carries, 103 yards, and one touchdown.

That one touchdown, though, did a lot to wash away Collins' disappointing and frustrating career at Georgia. His ten-yard scoring run came in his last game as a Bulldog, the 19-10 win over Georgia Tech in 1996. Until then, Collins had perhaps been most famous as the player who pulled a hamstring while running to fetch his laundry from the dryer.

But mere statistics don't tell the story of the man who played with a heavy heart that had nothing to do with hamstring pulls and failed expectations. While he was at Georgia, his unborn daughter died during a miscarriage. Collins' lone touchdown meant success for him and his daughter. That touchdown "was important to me," he said. "My little girl was up in the clouds looking at her dad. She was in my heart. When I scored, I said to myself that it was for her. It felt really good; there was a smile on my face."

Odell Collins walked off the field a winner, reminding us that success isn't always about the numbers.

Are you a successful person? Your answer, of course, depends upon how you define success. Is the measure of your success based on the number of digits in your bank balance, the square footage of your house, that title on your office door, the size of your boat?

Certainly the world determines success by wealth, fame, prestige, awards, and possessions. Our culture screams that life is all about gratifying your own needs and wants. If it feels good, do it. It's basically the Beach Boys' philosophy of life.

But all success of this type has one glaring shortcoming: You can't take it with you. Eventually, Daddy takes the T-bird away. Like life itself, all these things are fleeting.

A more rewarding and lasting way to approach success is through the spiritual rather than the physical. The goal becomes not money or backslaps by sycophants but eternal life spent with God. Success of that kind is forever.

Success demands singleness of purpose.

-- Vince Lombardi

Success isn't permanent, and failure isn't fatal -- unless you're talking about your relationship with God.

THOSE THINGS

Read Isaiah 55:6-13.

"My thoughts are not your thoughts, neither are your ways my ways" (v. 8).

Wade McGuire stood amid the wreckage of the locker room and his dreams.

He had broken his racket, busted a toilet, and propelled a water jug across the Henry Feild Stadium locker room. But worst of all, he had lost in the quarterfinals of the 1993 SEC men's tennis championships, putting the Bulldogs in jeopardy. So he asked himself in despair and anger, "This is what I came back for?" McGuire had, according to his coach, Manuel Diaz, "basically hit rock bottom."

After finishing as the NCAA singles runner-up in 1992, McGuire had put what was sure to be a lucrative professional career on hold to return for his senior season to try to lead the Bulldogs to their first NCAA championship since 1987.

McGuire had transferred to Georgia in 1989 and promptly blew out his right knee his first day in Athens. He missed all of the 1989-90 season and was slowed for most of the 1990-91 season. "A lot of people wrote me off after that," he said. "Totally forgot about me. That hurt."

But McGuire wasn't finished with his run of trouble. In 1991, he rolled a golf cart and broke his right ankle. "You get to the point where you start to think, 'When is this all going to end?'" he said. It was just one thing after another for McGuire.

You've probably had a few of "those things" in your own life: bad breaks that occur without regard to justice, morality, or fair play. You wonder if everything in life is random with events determined by a chance roll of some cosmic dice. Is there really somebody scripting all this with logic and purpose?

Yes, there is; God is the author of everything.

We know how it all began; we even know how it all will end. It's in God's book. The part we play in God's kingdom, though, is in the middle, and that part is still being written. God is the author, and his ways are different from ours. After all he's God and we are not. That's why we don't know what's coming our way, and why "those things" catch us by surprise and dismay us when they do occur.

What God asks of us is that we trust him. He knows everything will be all right for those who follow Jesus.

And as for Wade McGuire: Following his meltdown, he beat the No.-1 and the No.-2 ranked collegiate players back-to-back to lead the Dogs to the SEC championship. Suddenly, "those things" didn't matter anymore. "This year hasn't gone the way I thought it would. But . . . this is really what I came back for," he said.

Sometimes the calls go your way, and sometimes they don't.
-- Olympic Gold Medalist Dr. Dot Richardson

Life confounds us because, while we know the end and the beginning of God's great story, we are part of the middle, which God is still writing.

LANGUAGE BARRIER

Read Mark 16:9-20.

"Go into all the world and preach the good news to all creation" (v. 15).

Frank Ros was the starting middle linebacker and the team captain for the 1980 national champion football team. He was tough and strong, but at one time in his life, he cried regularly at school – because he couldn't talk to anybody.

Ros was born in Barcelona, Spain. When he was six, his family sailed to America. He heard his first words of English – "Good morning" – on the ship. His family settled in Greenville, S.C., where his father had found work as an engineer in a textile factory, and Ros entered elementary school there. And his nightmare began.

In Spain, he had started school when he was three and "learned a lot in a hurry." He could already multiply and do long division, for instance. All he could say, though, was "Good morning." "I would have traded all my advancement for the ability to communicate," he recalled. "All the kids looked at me like I was crazy. It was a lonely, confused feeling I won't ever forget. I cried. I cried because I couldn't communicate." The only thing he could understand was lunch -- "I figured that out" -- though at his first lunch break, he headed out the door for home before his teacher grabbed him and escorted him to the school lunchroom.

Young Frank Ros needed several months before he began to

solve the language barrier that kept him from talking to the students around him. He became reasonably fluent in English only in his middle grades. In sports, especially football, he found a way to communicate.

As Frank Ros' early life in America illustrates, language often erects a real barrier to understanding. Recall your overseas vacation, your call to a tech support number when you got someone who spoke English but didn't understand it, or your fender bender with a guy whose English was limited. Talking loud and waving your hands doesn't facilitate communication; it just makes you look weird.

Like many other aspects of life, faith has its jargon that can sometimes hinder understanding. Sanctification, justification, salvation, Advent, Communion with its symbolism of eating flesh and drinking blood – these and many other words have specific meanings to Christians that may be incomprehensible, confusing, and downright daunting to the newcomer or the seeker.

But the heart of Christianity's message centers on words that require no explanation: words such as hope, joy, love, purpose, and community. Their meanings are universal because people the world over seek them in their lives. Nobody speaks that language better than Jesus.

Kindness is the universal language that all people understand.
-- Legendary Florida A&M Coach Jake Gaither

Jesus speaks across all language barriers because his message of hope and meaning resounds with people everywhere.

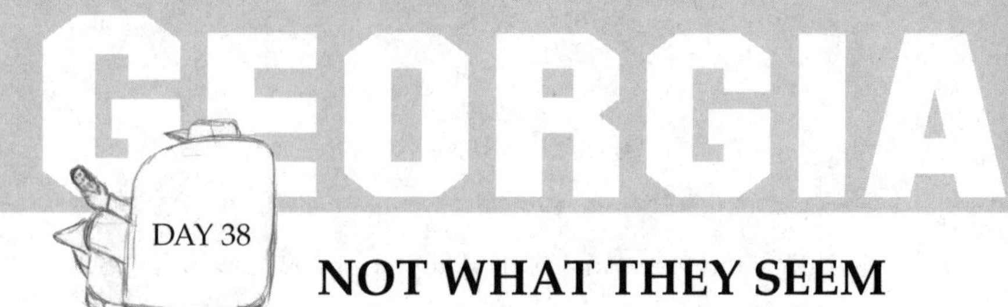

NOT WHAT THEY SEEM

Read Habakkuk 1:2-11.

"Why do you make me look at injustice? Why do you tolerate wrong? Destruction and violence are before me; there is strife, and conflict abounds" (v. 3).

The "Dream and Wonder Team" of 1927 with All-American ends Tom Nash and Chick Shiver opened the season with a 32-0 blasting of Virginia. Not surprisingly, though, Georgia was a big underdog the following weekend against mighty Yale in New Haven.

Each year Yale scheduled an intersectional game to give those without Yale connections a chance to see a game. Georgia was that intersectional game in 1927. Only 15,000 showed up, but a local radio station broadcast the game, and the crowd began to swell when Georgia refused to roll over and play dead.

Georgia took a 14-10 lead into the third quarter. Four times Yale crossed the Georgia 10, and four times they were denied. In the last minute of play, though, Yale apparently pulled out a miracle with a fourth-down pass completion. Two officials signaled touchdown. Yale had won. Or so it seemed.

During the week of the game, the field had been covered with hay to protect it from rain, and before the game the hay had been raked into piles at both ends of the field. Those piles partially obscured the goal lines.

The Yale receiver went down in one of those hay piles with

Georgia's Roy Estes on top of him. Estes grabbed hold of the receiver and refused to let him move until an official came over to see whether the Yale player had really crossed the goal line. When the official moved the hay aside, everyone saw the receiver was a yard short of the goal line. The touchdown was disallowed, and Georgia ran out the clock for a 14-10 upset win.

Sometimes in football things just aren't what they seem, and life is the same way. In our violent and convulsive times, we must confront the possibility of a new reality: that we are helpless in the face of anarchy; that injustice, destruction, and violence are pandemic in and symptomatic of our modern age. It seems that anarchy is winning, that the system of standards, values, and institutions we have cherished is crumbling while we watch.

But we should not be deceived or disheartened. God is in fact the arch-enemy of chaos, the creator of order and goodness and the architect of all of history. God is in control.

We often misinterpret history as the record of mankind's accomplishments -- which it isn't -- rather than the unfolding of God's plan -- which it is. That plan has a clearly defined end: God will make everything right. In that day things will be what they seem.

Unlike any other business in the United States, sports must preserve an illusion of perfect innocence.

-- Author Lewis H. Lapham

The forces of good and decency often seem helpless before evil's power, but don't be fooled: God is in control and will set things right.

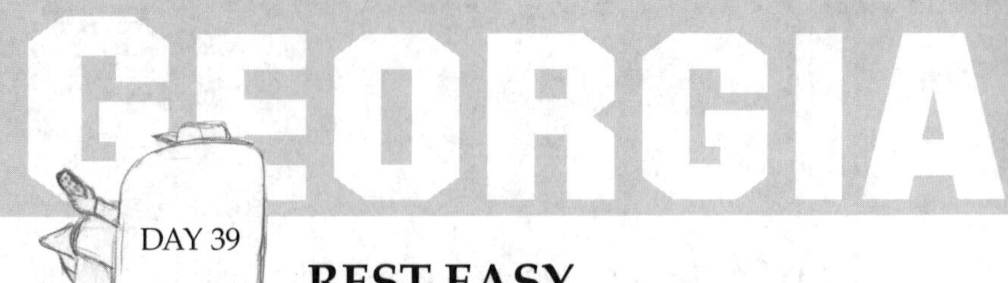

DAY 39

REST EASY

Read Hebrews 4:1-11.

"There remains, then, a Sabbath-rest for the people of God; for anyone who enters God's rest also rests from his own work, just as God did from his. Let us, therefore, make every effort to enter that rest" (vv. 9-11).

Angela Lettiere needed a break from tennis. What she got was a career-threatening injury.

Lettiere is among Georgia's greatest tennis players ever. In 2005, she was inducted into the Circle of Honor, the highest tribute UGA pays to its former athletes and coaches. In 1994, her senior year, Lettiere won the NCAA singles championship and led the Bulldog women to their first national championship. She and Michelle Anderson finished the year as the nation's top-ranked women's collegiate doubles team. She was named the SEC Player of the Year and the National Player of the Year and was All-America in both singles and doubles.

But after an All-American freshman season in 1991, she struggled as a sophomore. She was overweight and lost some of her speed. "I was absolutely too heavy," she admitted. "I wasn't in the shape I needed to be. . . . I was frustrated. I wasn't happy with myself. I felt like I needed rest. It got to the point where I just wasn't enjoying tennis."

She got more rest than she wanted. In a March 1992 match against William & Mary, her left knee popped with a torn ACL.

Many thought she was through, but instead, the down time rescued Lettiere's career. "It let me fall in love with tennis again," she said. "It made me realize how much I really do like playing the game."

Seven months later, she was back, better than ever -- because she had some time to rest. "I really do believe the injury was a blessing," Lettiere said.

As part of the natural rhythm of life, rest is important to maintain physical health. Rest has different images, though: a good eight hours in the sack; a Saturday morning that begins in the backyard with the paper and a pot of coffee; a vacation in the mountains, where the most strenuous thing you do is change position in the hot tub.

Rest is also part of the rhythm and the health of your spiritual life. Often we envision the faithful person as always busy, always doing something for God whether it's teaching Sunday school or showing up at church every time the doors open.

But God himself rested from work, and in blessing us with the Sabbath, he calls us into a time of rest. To rest by simply spending time in the presence of God is to receive spiritual revitalization and rejuvenation. Sleep refreshes your body and your mind; God's rest refreshes your soul.

Happiness is being able to lay your head on the pillow at night and sleep.

-- Herschel Walker

God promises you a spiritual rest that renews and refreshes your soul.

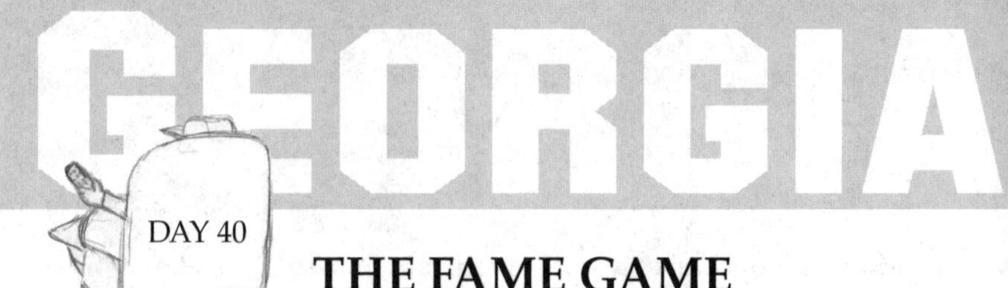

THE FAME GAME

Read 1 Kings 10:23-11:13.

"King Solomon was greater in riches and wisdom than all the other kings of the earth. The whole world sought audience with Solomon" (vv. 23-24).

Bob Hope, Errol Flynn, Bing Crosby, Ginger Rogers -- the 1942 Bulldogs hobnobbed with them all, and they even got into a spat with actress Rita Hayworth.

With Heisman-Trophy winner Frank Sinkwich, All-American end George Poschner, and several other all-stars, the Dogs were pretty well known themselves when they boarded a special train for Pasadena and a game with UCLA in the Rose Bowl. After an incident in Albuquerque, they were even more famous.

That's where they met fellow passenger Spencer Tracy, who said he didn't understand why the players were clustered around him when Rita Hayworth was around. Poschner and guard Harry Kuniansky needed no more encouragement to dash to Hayworth's compartment shouting "Telegram for Miss Hayworth."

When she opened the door, Poschner stuck his foot in it and refused to leave. The peeved starlet later related the story to famous Hollywood gossip columnist Hedda Hopper, who chastised the Bulldogs for their boorish behavior. Other columnists and some sports writers then rallied to the Bulldogs' side, and public sentiment turned against Hayworth, who invited the players to a Hollywood party as a way of making up. Coach Wally

Butts reluctantly allowed his players to go, but only after strictly forbidding any drinking.

The Dogs were the toast of Tinseltown, especially after they whipped UCLA 9-0. Georgia got a safety on a blocked punt from guard Red Boyd and a two-yard touchdown run from Sinkwich.

Have you ever wanted to be famous? Hanging out with other rich and famous people, having people listen to what you say, throwing money around like toilet paper, meeting adoring and clamoring fans, signing autographs, and posing for the paparazzi before you climb into your imported sports car?

Many of us yearn to be famous, well-known in the places and by the people that we believe matter. That's all fame amounts to: strangers knowing your name and your face.

The truth is that you are already famous where it really does matter, which excludes TV's talking heads, screaming teenagers, moviegoers, or D.C. power brokers. You are famous because Almighty God knows your name, your face, and everything about you. If a persistent photographer snapped you pondering this fame – the only kind that has eternal significance – would the picture show the world unbridled joy or the shell-shocked expression of a mug shot?

When you play a sport, you have two things in mind. One is to get into the Hall of Fame and the other is to go to heaven when you die.

– Lee Trevino

You're already famous because God knows your name and your face, which may be either reassuring or terrifying.

FATHER FIGURE

Read Matthew 3:13-17.

"A voice from heaven said, 'This is my Son, whom I love; with him I am well pleased'" (v. 17).

Freshman Mike Cavan was sitting around the dorm talking football with David McKnight, Brad Johnson, and Jake Scott, and he told them he started at quarterback in high school as a freshman. McKnight said, "What kind of dumb coach would start a true freshman at quarterback?" Cavan replied, "My dad."

Cavan quarterbacked the Dogs from 1968-70. He was the SEC Sophomore of the Year in 1968 and led the Dogs to the league championship that season. Having his dad, Jim, as his high school coach wasn't always easy for either of them. Cavan even went to his mother a couple of times to talk about quitting, but she always said no, that one day he would understand why his father was so tough on him. "When I got older and became a coach myself I did understand," he said. "We had some great times together. He died in 1983, and I still miss him a whole lot."

In December 1966, Cavan committed to Alabama, but when he told his dad of his decision, Jim said only one word: "No." Mike's answer was to bow his back; he said, "Fine, I'm not going anywhere." And his dad replied, "Fine, but you're not going to Alabama." On into January, Mike still hadn't signed with anybody, and "it dawned on me that Daddy was not going to budge on this particular issue." So he signed with Georgia, and "Daddy was right. But then again, he was just about always right." Going to Georgia, Cavan said, "was the best decision I ever made, or I should say had made for me."

American society largely belittles and marginalizes fathers and their influence upon their sons. Men are perceived as necessary to effect pregnancy; after that, they can leave and everybody's better off.

But we need look in only two places to appreciate the enormity of that misconception: our jails – packed with males who lacked the influence of fathers in their lives as they grew up -- and the Bible. God – being God – could have chosen any relationship he desired between Jesus and himself, including society's approach of irrelevancy.

Instead, the most important relationship in all of history was that of father-son. God obviously believes a close, loving relationship between fathers and sons, such as that of Jim and Mike Cavan, is crucial. For men and women to espouse otherwise or for men to walk blithely and carelessly out of their children's lives constitutes disobedience to the divine will.

Simply put, God loves fathers. After all, he is one.

My dad was a huge influence on me. I imagine if he had put a wrench in my hand I would have been a great mechanic.

-- Pete Maravich

**Fatherhood is a tough job,
but a model for the father-child relationship is
found in that of Jesus the Son with God the Father.**

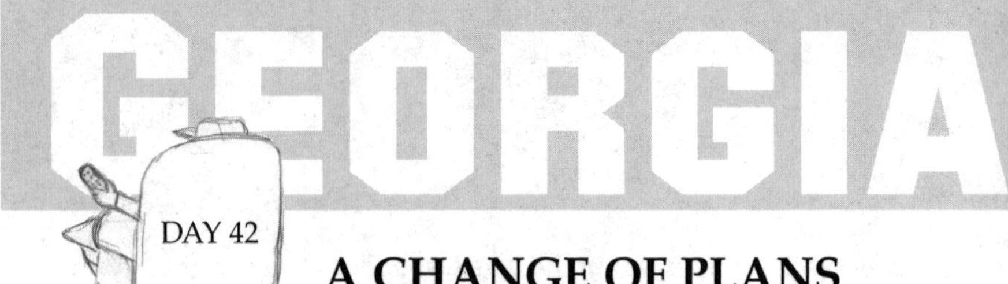

A CHANGE OF PLANS

Read Genesis 18:20-33.

"The Lord said, 'If I find fifty righteous people in the city of Sodom, I will spare the whole place for their sake'" (v. 26).

The 1983 basketball Dogs made a miraculous run to the Final Four, but they got past the first round because they had a change of plans in the final seconds.

The SEC tournament champions began their run in Greensboro, N.C., against Virginia Commonwealth, the champions of the Sun Belt Conference. Coach Hugh Durham knew his Dogs "were an experienced team, but we weren't experienced in NCAA Tournament play." Senior forward James Banks reinforced Durham's point: "This was our first time playing in the big boys' tournament." So Durham told his team, "The most difficult game of the NCAA Tournament is always the first one."

He was right about this one. Georgia led 50-41 with 11:31 to play but then went seven minutes without scoring. The drought left the teams tied at 54 with 90 seconds left. VCU held the ball for the last shot in this era before the shot clock, but Banks and Vern Fleming forced a turnover. Georgia now prepared for one last shot.

"We wanted to run a pattern that would give us two or three options," Durham said as he instructed his players on exactly what they should do. And the whole thing fell apart. The play completely broke down as the clock ticked away. With time running out and the ball in his hands, Banks improvised. He faked his defender and put up a jumper from the free-throw line. The ball sat interminably on the rim before deciding to fall in.

The Dogs had a change of plans, won the game, and were on their way to the Final Four.

To be unable to adapt to changing circumstances to is stultify and die. It's true of animal life, of business and industry, of the military, of sports teams in pressure-packed situations, of you and your relationships, your job, and your finances.

Changing your plans regularly therefore is rather routine for you. But consider how remarkable it is that the God of the universe may change his mind about something. What could bring that about?

Prayer. Someone -- whether it's an old nomad named Abraham or a 21st-century Bulldog fan like you -- talks to God, who listens and considers what is asked of him.

You may feel uncomfortable praying. Maybe you're reluctant and embarrassed; perhaps you feel you're not very good at it. But nobody majors in prayer at school, and as for being reluctant, what have you got to lose? Your answer may even be a change of plans on God's part. Such is the power of prayer.

There are two things you can do with your head down: play golf and pray.

-- Lee Trevino

Prayer is powerful;
it may even change God's mind.

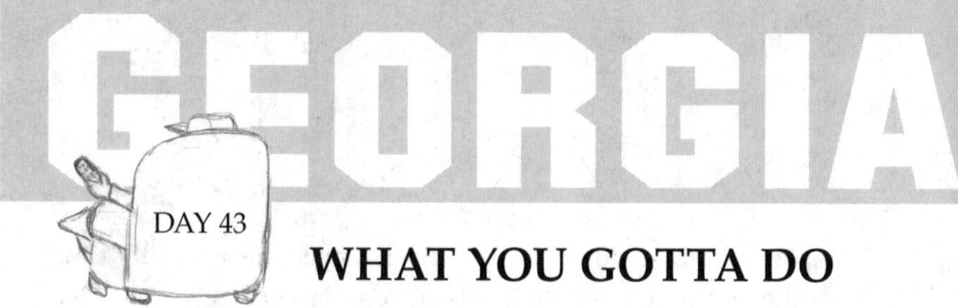

WHAT YOU GOTTA DO

Read 2 Samuel 12:1-14.

"The Lord sent Nathan to David" (v. 1).

Lindsay Scott didn't want to tell Tennessee no.

The Jesup wide receiver, who was to be a key component of Georgia's 1980 national championship and in Jacksonville would be half of the most famous throw-and-catch in Georgia football history, actually committed to the Vols. The Tennessee coaches made a strategic mistake, though, when they told Scott not to sign on signing day so head coach Johnny Majors could be present.

The extra days gave Scott time to question his decision, and Georgia coach Mike Cavan acted on a hunch he had: that Scott wanted to sign with Georgia but didn't know how to tell the Tennessee coaches. So on Christmas Eve 1977, Cavan flew down to Jesup and spent Christmas in a motel room. Upon seeing him in town, Scott said, "Coach Cavan, you're crazy."

The day after Christmas Cavan and coach Wayne McDuffie showed up at the Scott house at 6:30 a.m. to see two Tennessee coaches walking in the front door. "The battle of nerves, of recruiting cat-and-mouse, was on." Three hours passed with both sets of coaches waiting before an anxious Cavan finally strode into Scott's bedroom. He had been right. Scott wanted to sign with Georgia, but he didn't want to face the UT coaches. Cavan said, "You've got to go out there and tell those people what you are going to do. You gotta tell 'em you've made up your mind and you're going to Georgia and that's final."

Scott agreed, and the tension was heavy as he walked into his living room. He took a deep breath and said, "I've thought it over, and I've decided the best thing for me to do is to go to the University of Georgia."

Lindsay Scott had done it.

Just as Lindsay Scott had to, you've had to do some things in your life that you really didn't want to do. Maybe when you put your daughter on severe restriction, broke the news of a death in the family, fired a friend, or underwent surgery. You plowed ahead because you knew it was for the best or you had no choice.

Nathan surely didn't want to confront King David and tell him what a miserable reprobate he'd been, but the prophet had no choice: Obedience to God overrode all other factors. Of all that God asks of us in the living of a godly life, obedience is perhaps the most difficult. After all, our history of disobedience stretches all the way back to the Garden of Eden.

The problem is that God expects obedience not only when his wishes match our own but also when they don't. Obedience to God is a way of life, not a matter of convenience.

Coaching is making men do what they don't want, so they can become what they want to be.

-- Legendary NFL Coach Tom Landry

You can never foresee what God will demand of you, but obedience requires being ready to do whatever God asks.

DAY 44

SOUTHERN HOSPITALITY

Read 2 Kings 4:8-17.

"Let's make a small room on the roof and put in it a bed and a table, a chair and a lamp for him. Then he can stay there whenever he comes to us" (v. 10).

Imagine the Arch draped in the opponents' colors and nobody getting upset!

On Oct. 12, 1929, "such an epidemic of Southern hospitality raged that students did not rebel when their famed Arch was draped in blue instead of the beloved red and black." The blue was for the Bulldogs of Yale, coming to Athens for the Sanford Stadium dedicatory game. For the special occasion, "hundreds of flags waved welcome to thousands of visitors, and streets, stores, and mansions featured football decorations blending Yale Blue and Georgia Red and Black."

Dr. Steadman Sanford, the father of Sanford Stadium, "had induced Yale to make its first appearance on a football field below the Mason and Dixon line." Sanford had pursued Yale for the big day because of UGA's close ties to the New Haven school. A Yale alumnus, Abraham Baldwin, had written the university's charter and a Yale man had designed the stadium.

A carnival atmosphere prevailed in Athens on this day that marked the beginning of big-time football at UGA. The Yale team, the band, and their fans arrived by train, and they got a taste of Southern hospitality when thousands welcomed them by singing the Yale "Boola Boola" fight song. Georgia's male senior class then escorted the guests to their headquarters, the Georgian Hotel. Along the way, the Yale Band contributed to the bedlam by breaking into "Glory, Glory" to Old Georgia.

The only time Georgia proved to be rather inhospitable was on that brand new field in that brand new stadium. The Dogs upset the heavily favored Yalies 15-0 as Vernon "Catfish" Smith became an instant legend by scoring all 15 points.

Southerners are deservedly famous for their hospitality. Down South, warmth and genuineness seem genetic. You open your home to the neighborhood kids, to your friends, to the stranger whose car broke down in the rain, to the stray cat that showed up hungry and hollering, to displaced family members.

Hospitality was vital to the cultures of Biblical times also. Travelers faced innumerable dangers: everything from lions to bandits to deadly desert heat. Finding a temporary haven thus often became quite literally a matter of life and death.

Since hospitality has through the ages been a sign of a loving and generous nature, it is not surprising that almighty God himself is a gracious host. He welcomes you, not as a stranger, but as an adopted child. One glorious day this hospitable God will open the doors of his place for you -- and never ask you to leave.

Being raised in the South means growing up on a diet of southern hospitality and a dose of football every weekend.

– Askman.com

Hospitality is an outward sign of the inward loving, generous, and godly nature of the host.

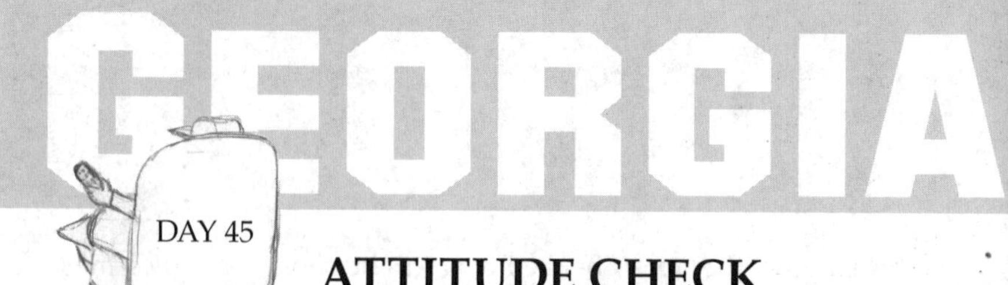

DAY 45

ATTITUDE CHECK

Read 1 Thessalonians 5.

"Give thanks in all circumstances, for this is God's will for you in Christ Jesus" (v. 18).

"You'll never do anything at Georgia. There's no support there."

That's the warning Suzanne Yoculan received in 1983 when she was considering becoming the coach of the Georgia women's gymnastics team. Under the circumstances, it wasn't bad advice.

The athletic department was discussing eliminating the program. The team had enjoyed little success, had never won an SEC championship, had not even qualified for the first two NCAA championships, and routinely drew fewer than 200 fans to a home meet. Most of those faithful followers were "the gymnasts' boyfriends, roommates, and families."

The facilities weren't much. The women shared practice space with the men's team (since discontinued) in a 1920s-era gym in the old women's physical education building. Yoculan's office was a cubicle in the old trophy room of the Coliseum, which was jammed with about fifteen other coaches. It was so noisy Yoculan had to come back at night to call recruits on the phone; otherwise, they couldn't hear her.

And yet she built the most successful program in UGA athletic history with the highest winning percentage of any female college coach in any sport. When she retired after the 2009 season, her teams had won ten national championships, 16 SEC titles, and 21 regional championships. What led her to take the job in the first place? What carried her through those daunting early days?

Her attitude. "To me, it was wonderful," Yoculan said. "It was an office. It was a place to work, and it provided an opportunity to do something and make something happen. I didn't see any negatives at all when I first came here."

How's your attitude? You can fuss because your house is not as big as some, because a coworker talks too much, or because you have to take pills every day. Or you can appreciate your home for providing warmth and shelter, the co-worker for the lively conversation, and the medicine for keeping you reasonably healthy.

Whether life is endured or enjoyed depends largely on your attitude. An attitude of thankfulness to God offers you the best chance to get the most out of your life because living in gratitude means you choose joy in your life no matter what your circumstances may be.

This world does not exist for your benefit or to satisfy you, so the odds are pretty good that it will do neither. True contentment and joy are found in a deep, abiding relationship with God, and the proper way to approach God is not with haughtiness or anger but with gratitude for all he has given you.

An awesome attitude is best described as a "bad case of the wants."
– Erk Russell

Your attitude goes a long way toward determining the quality of your life and your relationship with God.

DAY 46

TOWEL THROWERS

Read Numbers 13:25-14:4.

"The men who had gone up with him said, 'We can't attack those people; they are stronger than we are'" (v. 13:31).

Georgia once kept an All-American center because he couldn't find his way to New Jersey.

In 1985, Peter Anderson became the first player ever so honored by Coach Vince Dooley when he was named a team captain in the middle of the season. The senior also was All-America that season.

In high school, though, Anderson didn't really know much about college football. One of his teammates had to explain to him "who Herschel Walker was and the significance of being recruited by a place like Georgia." Rutgers was the only other school recruiting him; with their facilities and their 15,000 fans stacked against Georgia's 85,000-plus fanatics, "It just wasn't a fair comparison," Anderson said.

When he came to Athens in 1981 from New Jersey, Anderson discovered a team loaded with offensive linemen. A long way from home with little apparent chance of playing, he decided to quit, pack his bags, and head back to Jersey when he didn't dress out for the season opener against Tennessee, a 44-0 Georgia win.

As Anderson told it, he left town in "this big Oldsmobile Delta 88, and I had no idea where I was going. I had to pull into a gas station at 2:00 in the morning and talk this guy into taking my check to fill up the tank." Anderson also had no idea where he was and had a sneaking suspicion he hadn't even made it out of the state yet. "I realized I wasn't going to make it to Jersey that night, so I turned around and went back to Athens. It's a good thing I did."

A good thing indeed that Peter Anderson tried to quit but couldn't.

Remember that time you quit a high-school sports team? Bailed out of a relationship? Walked away from that job with the goals unachieved? Sometimes quitting is the most sensible way to minimize your losses, so you may well at times in your life give up on something or someone.

In your relationship with God, however, you should remember the people of Israel, who quit when the Promised Land was theirs for the taking. They forgot one fact of life you never should: God never gives up on you.

That means you should never, ever give up on God. No matter how tired or discouraged you get, no matter that it seems your prayers aren't getting through to God, no matter what – quitting on God is not an option. He is preparing a blessing for you, and in his time, he will bring it to fruition -- if you don't quit on him.

The first time you quit, it's hard. The second time, it gets easier. The third time, you don't even have to think about it.

-- Bear Bryant

Whatever else you give up on in your life, don't give up on God; he will never ever give up on you.

THE SCAPEGOAT

Read Leviticus 16:15-22.

"He is to lay both hands on the head of the live goat and confess over it all the wickedness and rebellion of the Israelites—all their sins—and put them on the goat's head" (v. 21).

Back before there was a bulldog named Uga, back before there was a bulldog at all, there was a goat.

The University of Georgia's first football game – and the first intercollegiate football game in the Deep South – was played against Mercer on Jan. 30, 1892. The *Athens Banner* reported that the "Mercer boys came in at twelve o'clock and brought with them two cars full of students and citizens of Macon, Madison, and other places along the line of the Macon and Northern."

The Georgia mascot for the game was a goat. The goat may not at first have been a serious mascot because the pre-game festivities included the goat's being driven across the field by a band of students, which "raised quite a ripple of laughter." After the 50-0 Georgia win, the *Banner* said, "Enthusiasm was supreme. . . . The boys were riding around on a sea of shoulders. Even the goat was ridden."

The goat made the trip to Atlanta for the Auburn game of Feb. 20. As the *Atlanta Journal* put it in its pre-game preview, the "mascot goat will be along. This goat, draped in college colors . . . has been a requisite part of the paraphernalia of the football team." Sure enough, the goat showed up at Piedmont Park, gaily bedecked in a black coat or blanket with red letters – "U" and "G" – on each side and a hat with red and black ribbons. The goat was "enthusiastically applauded."

A couple of seasons later, the UGA mascot was a solid white bull terrier owned by a student, and the goat disappeared into history – or into a barbecue pit.

A particular type of goat -- a scapegoat – could really be useful. Mess up at work? Bring him in to get chewed out. Make a decision your children don't like? Let her put up with the whining and complaining. Forget your anniversary? Call him in to grovel and explain.

What a set-up! You don't have to pay the price for your mistakes, your shortcomings, and your failures. You get off scot-free. Exactly the way forgiveness works with Jesus.

Our sins separate us from God because we the unholy can't stand in the presence of the holy God. To remove our guilt, God requires a blood sacrifice. Out of his unimaginable love for us, he provided the sacrifice – his own son. Jesus is the sacrifice made for us; through Jesus and Jesus alone, forgiveness and eternity with God are ours. It's a bumper sticker, but it's true: We aren't perfect; we're just forgiven.

I never blame myself when I'm not hitting. I just blame the bat, and if it keeps up, I change bats.

– Yogi Berra

For all those times you fail God, you have Jesus to take the guilt and the blame for you.

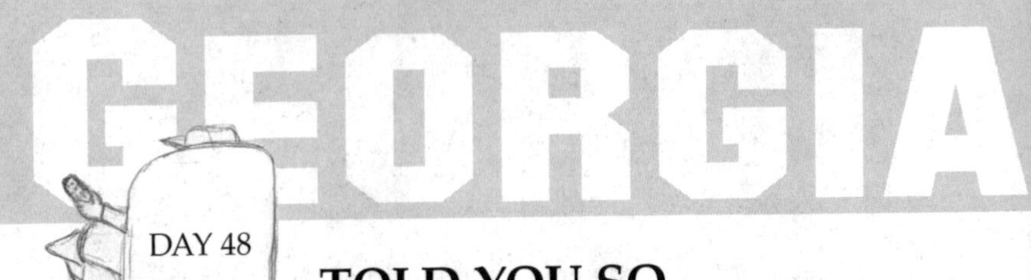

DAY 48

TOLD YOU SO

Read Matthew 24:15-31.

"See, I have told you ahead of time" (v. 25).

A lot of people at all levels of play told Fran Tarkenton he couldn't make it in football.

Tarkenton once said, "I have never really been able to persuade many people right out of the blocks . . . that I belonged in the front row in football. . . . The number of nonbelievers in Francis Tarkenton in football has been very impressive, and you might say even scary."

UGA head coach Wally Butts, for instance, "was the first in a long line of brilliant football minds who didn't think Francis Tarkenton had much of a future as a professional football player." Butts did concede that Tarkenton had at best "a reasonable chance of lettering at Georgia, eventually."

Tarkenton didn't even start one of the most famous games in UGA history: the last-minute 14-13 win over Auburn that clinched the 1959 SEC championship. But he was in at the finish, hitting Bill Herron in the left corner of the end zone on fourth down from the thirteen. And Tarkenton said the legend is true: He drew up the game-winning play in the huddle.

Tarkenton was All-SEC in 1959 and 1960 and All-America in 1960; nevertheless, he was not drafted into the NFL until the third round. As Tarkenton put it, "All the first-rate college quarterbacks

. . . were automatic first-round choices." But not him.

Despite the naysayers, he went on to play 18 seasons in the NFL and is a member of both the college football and the pro football halls of fame. Late in his career, Tarkenton ran into Butts, who said, "I think you're the best quarterback in football today."

Francis Tarkenton could have said it, but he didn't: "I told you so."

Don't you just hate it in when somebody says, "I told you so"? That means the other person was right and you were wrong; that other person has spoken the truth. You could have listened to that know-it-all in the first place, but then you would have lost the chance yourself to crow, "I told you so."

In our pluralistic age and society, many view truth as relative, meaning absolute truth does not exist. All belief systems have equal value and merit. But this is a ghastly, dangerous fallacy because it ignores the truth that God proclaimed in the presence and words of Jesus.

In speaking the truth, Jesus told everybody exactly what he was going to do: come back and take his faithful with him. Those who don't listen or who don't believe will be left behind with those four awful words, "I told you so," ringing in their ears and wringing their souls.

There's nothing in this world more instinctively abhorrent to me than finding myself in agreement with my fellow humans.

-- Lou Holtz

Jesus matter-of-factly told us what he has planned: He will return to gather all the faithful to himself.

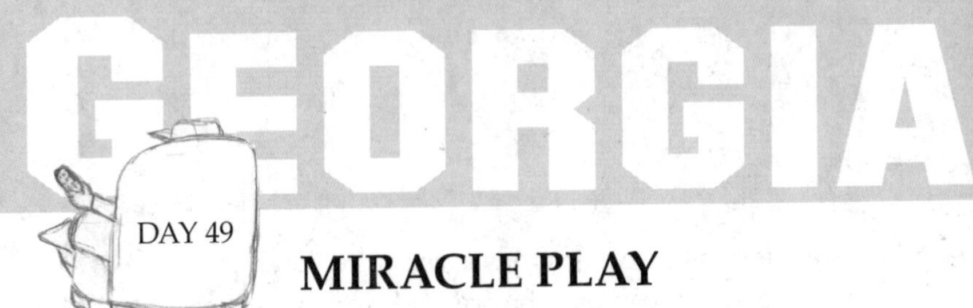

MIRACLE PLAY

Read Matthew 12:38-42.

"He answered, 'A wicked and adulterous generation asks for a miraculous sign!'" (v. 39)

Losing your last five games of the season means you need a break just to get into the postseason and a downright miracle to win a championship. But the baseball Dogs of 1990 got the break and pulled off the miracle.

Throughout most of the regular season, the Dogs were one of the best in the nation, rolling up a 42-10 record with only seven games left to play. That's when they decided to play their worst baseball of the season, losing the SEC title to LSU on the last day of the season and then being ignominiously ousted from the SEC tournament with two straight losses.

Despite that collapse, the NCAA awarded the 44-17 Dogs a berth as the number two seed in the Northeast Regional in Waterbury, Conn. That was the break they needed; now came the miracles. The Dogs disposed of Connecticut, Maine, North Carolina, and Rutgers to claim a berth in the College World Series.

Behind All-American Dave Fleming, the fourth-seeded Dogs shut out Mississippi State 3-0 in the opening round. Next up was top-seeded Stanford and a game that will forever be part of Bulldog baseball lore. Mike Rebhan pitched a five-hitter, and Georgia tied a World Series record by scoring 11 runs in the sixth inning to defeat Mike Mussina.

In a rematch, Rebhan beat Mussina again, 5-1, propelling the Miracle Dawgs into the championship game against heavily favored Oklahoma State. Freshman lefty Stan Payne went six innings, and Fleming mopped up as Georgia finished the miracle run to the national championship with a 2-1 win.

Miracles defy rational explanation. Like winning a national championship after closing the season with five straight losses. Or escaping with minor abrasions from an accident that totals your car. Or recovering from an illness that seemed terminal. Underlying the notion of miracles is that they are rare instances of direct divine intervention that reveal God.

But life shows us quite the contrary, that miracles are anything but rare. Since God made the world and everything in it, everything around you is miraculous. Even you are a miracle.

Your life can be mundane, dull, ordinary, and tiresome, or it can be spent in a glorious attitude of childlike wonder and awe. It depends on whether or not you see the world through the eyes of faith; only through faith can you discern the hand of God in any event. Only through faith can you see the miraculous and thus see God.

Jesus knew that miracles don't produce faith, but rather faith produces miracles.

Do you believe in miracles? Yes!
– Broadcaster Al Michaels when U.S. defeated USSR in hockey in 1980 Winter Games.

Miracles are all around us,
but it takes the eyes of faith to see them.

DAY 50

GOOD SPORT

Read Titus 2:1-8.

"Show integrity, seriousness and soundness of speech that cannot be condemned, so that those who oppose you may be ashamed because they have nothing bad to say about us" (vv. 7b, 8).

He got his nickname because he once won a bet against some high school buddies by biting off the head of an Ocmulgee River catfish. In addition to his colorful moniker, he was one of Georgia's greatest athletes and a good sport to boot.

He was Vernon "Catfish" Smith.

Catfish is part of Georgia legend for scoring all 15 points as Georgia upset powerhouse Yale 15-0 in the 1929 dedicatory game of Sanford Stadium. He caught a touchdown pass from Spurgeon Chandler, kicked the extra point, tackled a Yale runner for a safety, and recovered a blocked punt in the end zone for Georgia's second touchdown. Smith was an All-Southern Conference end for three years and was All-America in 1931, his senior season. He was inducted into the College Football Hall of Fame in 1979.

But Catfish was also a pretty good basketball and baseball player, and in the finals of the Southern Conference basketball tournament in 1932 against North Carolina, he demonstrated his sportsmanship. Georgia's star center, Bill Strickland, had sprained an ankle, so Smith moved from forward to center for the game.

UGA held a 26-24 lead with only ten seconds to play when

Smith stole the ball and broke wide open down the floor. Two Tarheels promptly knocked him "clear off the court" just as the gun sounded to end the game. Instead of retaliating, Smith simply picked himself up and turned to shake hands with the Carolina team captain. He even declined to shoot the free throws, letting the score stand as it was.

One of life's paradoxes is that many who would never consider cheating on the tennis court or the racquetball court to gain an advantage think nothing of doing so in other areas of their life. In other words, the good sportsmanship they practice on the golf course or even on the Monopoly board doesn't carry over. They play with the truth, cut corners, abuse others verbally, run roughshod over the weaker, and generally cheat whenever they can to gain an advantage on the job or in their personal relationships.

But good sportsmanship is a way of living, not just of playing. Shouldn't you accept defeat without complaint (You don't have to like it.); win gracefully without gloating; treat your competition with fairness, courtesy, generosity, and respect?

That's the way one team treats another in the name of sportsmanship. That's the way one person treats another in the name of Jesus.

One person practicing sportsmanship is better than a hundred teaching it.

-- Knute Rockne

Sportsmanship -- treating others with courtesy, fairness, and respect -- is a way of living, not just a way of playing.

DON'T SAY GOOD-BYE

Read John 13:33-38.

"My children, I will be with you only a little longer" (v. 33a).

They had seen it many times before, but on this night the Georgia crowd stood on its feet and cheered. They knew that they had seen it for perhaps the last time and that soon, no one would ever see it again.

"It" went like this: Kelly Miller – Georgia's first two-time SEC Player of the Year and a two-time All-America -- barely looked up before she heaved a half-court pass. A wide-open Coco Miller – like Kelly a unanimous choice for All-SEC in 2001 -- made the catch a step or two away from the basket right where Kelly knew she would be, bounced the basketball once, and laid it up for two.

How can they do that? "We've played with each other so long that I knew she would get down there," Kelly said.

But what they had came from something more than playing together, for they were the Miller twins of Georgia women's basketball legend. "It's kind of freaky, I guess," Coco said.

This particular occasion was the last home game of the 2000-2001 season. The most celebrated and accomplished twins in collegiate basketball history were seniors; their collegiate playing days were over except for the SEC and NCAA tournaments. Soon the Miller twins would be drafted into the WNBA, and for the first time in their lives, they would not be playing together or living together.

"I can't imagine ever playing without Kelly," Coco said.

But the time came for them to say good-bye. Kelly went to Charlotte, Coco to Washington, D.C. Even for twins who are basketball All-Americas, good-byes are inevitable in life.

You've stood on the curb and watched someone you love drive off, or you've grabbed a last-minute hug before a plane leaves. Maybe it was a child leaving home for the first time or your best friends moving halfway across the country. It's an extended – maybe even permanent – separation, and good-byes hurt.

Jesus felt the pain of parting too. Throughout his brief ministry, Jesus had been surrounded by and had depended upon his friends and confidantes, the disciples. About to leave them, he gathered them for a going-away supper and gave them a heads-up about what was about to happen.

In the process, he offered them words of comfort. What a wonderful friend he was! Even though he was the one who was about to suffer unimaginable agony, Jesus' concern was for the pain his friends would feel.

But Jesus wasn't just saying good-bye. He was about his mission of providing the way through which none of us would ever have to say good-bye again.

They say money talks. The only thing it says to me is good-bye.
– Baseball Hall of Famer Paul Waner

Through Jesus, we will see the day when we say good-bye to good-byes.

GEORGIA

DAY 52

THE RIGHT PERSON

Read Matthew 26:47-50; 27:1-10.

"The betrayer had arranged a signal with them: 'The one I kiss is the man; arrest him.' Going at once to Jesus, Judas said, 'Greetings, Rabbi!' and kissed him" (vv. 48-49).

Erk Russell practically had to beg Vince Dooley to give him a job.

Immediately after he was hired on Dec. 5, 1963, to resurrect the moribund Georgia football program, Dooley set about assembling his first coaching staff. He did so in careful consultation with his boss, Athletic Director Joel Eaves. Among the ten hires Dooley made was his brother Bill, who came from Mississippi State as the offensive coordinator.

Dooley and Eaves agreed that a vital step would be hiring some coaches with previous ties to Georgia. This was accomplished by luring former Bulldog assistant coach Sterling Dupree away from Florida to lock up recruiting in the state.

In late January, though, the key position of defensive coordinator remained to be filled. One particular coach was actively seeking the job: a guy named Erk Russell. Russell had spent a year at Vanderbilt as defensive coordinator. Both Auburn alums, Dooley and he had coached together at their alma mater. As writer Tim Hix put it, Dooley didn't exactly run up to Nashville and implore Russell to come to Athens. "Rather, it was Russell who did much of the begging." "He didn't exactly break my door down," Erk said. "I did call him on several occasions to say, 'Hey, Vince, how 'bout a job?'"

Most Georgia fans would agree with Hix, who proclaimed Russell the best hire Dooley ever made. Dooley agreed, declaring Erk "the cornerstone of our coaching staff for seventeen years." He was also the most beloved assistant coach in Georgia history.

As Bulldog lore and legend reveal, Erk Russell was the right man for the job.

What do you want to be when you grow up, whenever that is? Somehow you are supposed to know the answer to that question when you're a teenager, the time in life when common sense and logic are at their lowest ebb.

Long after those halcyon teen years are left behind, you may make frequent career changes. You chase the job that gives you not just financial rewards but also some personal satisfaction and sense of accomplishment. You desire a profession that uses your abilities, that you enjoy doing, and that gives you a sense of contributing to something bigger than yourself.

God, too, wants you in the right job, one that he has designed specifically for you. After all, even Judas was the right man for what God needed done. To do his work, God gave you abilities, talents, and passions. Do what you do best and what you love -- just do it for God.

It's work to keep your name out of the papers regarding other jobs.
-- Vince Dooley

God has a job for you, one for which he gave you particular talents, abilities, and passions.

RESPECTFULLY YOURS

Read Mark 8:31-38.

"He then began to teach them that the Son of Man must suffer many things and be rejected by the elders, chief priests and teachers of the law, and that he must be killed" (v. 31).

Georgia's football recruits assume – rightly so -- that they will be playing for a school whose program is nationally respected. But it wasn't always that way.

In the 1940s, a player from Ohio helped Georgia football earn a national reputation for excellence. "That guy Spankovich is at it again," declared an exasperated Georgia Tech PA announcer during the 1939 freshman game at Grant Field. "Spankovich" was in reality Frank Sinkwich.

In 1941, Sinkwich set an SEC rushing record with 1,103 yards and a conference total offense record with 1,816 yards. He was named All-America and finished fourth in the Heisman Trophy balloting. The 8-1-1 Dogs went to the Orange Bowl where Sinkwich gained national headlines with 382 yards of total offense and four touchdowns in a 40-26 romp over TCU.

His senior season, Sinkwich led Georgia to a 9-1 record and a 9-0 win over UCLA in the 1942 Rose Bowl. The Bulldogs were consensus national champions. Sinkwich was named All-America a second time, and he became the first player from a southern school to win the Heisman Trophy.

A magazine article in the 1950s asserted that Sinkwich at that time was the best offensive player in the history of college football and used Sinkwich's gaudy statistics to back up its point.

For the University of Georgia, though, Sinkwich was bigger than his individual achievements. "Through his performances in high-profile games, Sinkwich forced the rest of the country to pay attention to Georgia football for the first time." "He put us on the map," Dan Magill said.

Rodney Dangerfield made a good living as a comedian with a repertoire that was basically only countless variations on one punch line: "I don't get no respect." Dangerfield was successful because he struck a chord with his audience. No one wants to play football for a program that no one respects. You want the respect, the esteem, and the regard that you feel you've earned.

But more often than not, you don't get it. Still, you shouldn't feel too badly; you're in good company. In the ultimate example of disrespect, Jesus – the very Son of God -- was treated as the worst type of criminal. He was arrested, bound, scorned, ridiculed, spit upon, tortured, condemned, and executed.

God allowed his son to undergo such treatment because of his high regard and his love for you. You are respected by almighty God! Could anyone else's respect really matter?

The Georgia program makes you respect yourself both as an athlete and as a student.

-- Herschel Walker

You may not get the respect you deserve,
but at least nobody's spitting on you
and driving nails into you as they did to Jesus.

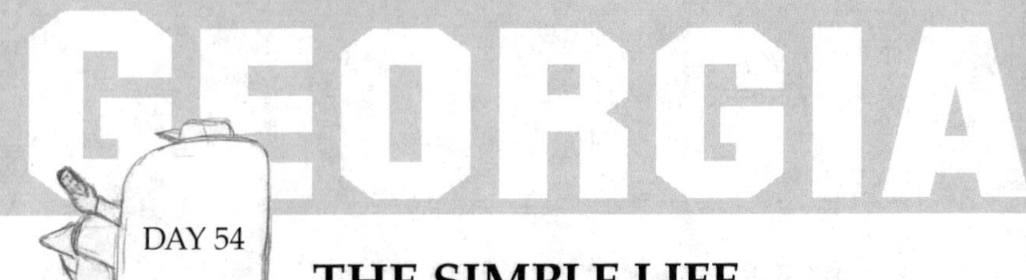

THE SIMPLE LIFE

Read 1 John 1:5-10.

"If we confess our sins, he is faithful and just and will forgive us our sins and purify us from all unrighteousness" (v. 9).

The formula for success in women's fast-pitch softball is pretty simple: Get yourself an ace pitcher and send her out to the mound until she can't pitch anymore. For Georgia softball coach Lu Harris-Champer, that formula meant Michelle Green.

Green, who joined the Georgia staff as an assistant coach in 2006, is the greatest pitcher in Georgia softball history. One writer said Green "gobbled up innings and wins like the old arcade game PacMan." As Green put it, "In the long run, I want to be the person out there." A knee injury in the middle of the 2004 season slowed her down somewhat, but still the records she set at Georgia during her career from 2002-05 are astounding.

Green holds the following records: season and career innings pitched (292 and 789), season and career wins (39 and 104), career ERA (1.30), game, season, and career strikeouts (17, 407, and 1070), and season and career shutouts (19.5 and 47.5). Her 2003 season was nothing short of phenomenal; she compiled a 39-8 record with a 1.10 ERA. Needless to say, the accolades poured in. She was a two-time All-America and All-SEC and twice was the SEC Pitcher of the Year.

So did the formula work for the team? During her four years

on the mound, the Dogs won two SEC titles and went to four straight NCAA tournaments.

Michelle Green let Lu Harris-Champer keep it simple. "We just have a tendency to go with what's working, and this seems to be working," Champer said. And the Dogs kept winning.

Perhaps the simple life in America was doomed by the arrival of the programmable VCR. Since then, we've been on an inevitably downward spiral into ever more complicated lives. Even windshield wipers have different settings now, and it takes a graduate degree to figure out clothes dryers.

But we might all do well in our own lives to mimic the UGA approach to softball while Michelle Green was in town. That is, we should approach our lives with the keen awareness that success requires simplicity, a sticking to the basics: Revere God, love our family, honor our country, do our best.

Theologians may make what God did in Jesus as complicated as quantum mechanics and the infield fly rule, but God kept it simple for us: believe, trust, and obey. Believe in Jesus as the Son of God, trust that through him God makes possible our deliverance from our sins into Heaven, and obey God in the way he wants us to live.

It's simple, but it's the way to win for all eternity.

I think God made it simple. Just accept Him and believe.

-- Bobby Bowden

Life continues to get ever more complicated,
but God made it simple for us
when he showed up as Jesus.

THE GOOD OLD DAYS

Read Psalm 102.

"My days vanish like smoke; . . . but you remain the same, and your years will never end" (vv. 3, 27).

How we do sometimes yearn for the good old days when folks cheered the Dogs on from the railroad tracks and freshmen were required to ring the chapel bell.

Never mind that they were freeloaders, the "Track People," watching games without paying. For decades, they were part of the charm of Georgia's home games, those denizens of the Central of Georgia railroad tracks that overlooked the east end of the stadium. They first showed up in 1929, the year Sanford Stadium opened for business, and kept coming, perched precariously atop the railroad tracks and edging aside when a train showed up.

In, 1981, though, they disappeared forever when Sanford's east end was enclosed and double decked, permanently blocking the view and upping the capacity to more than 82,000 -- paying customers all.

The Track People are part of history, our warm memories, and the good old days.

Once upon a time in the good old days, freshmen students were required to ring the Chapel bell until midnight after a Georgia win and all night long following a win over Georgia Tech.

That tradition is part of the good old days now, but students, alumni, and fans still rush to the Chapel to ring the bell after the

Dogs win. They did so on Oct. 27, 2007, after the 42-30 win over Florida with such enthusiasm that the yoke holding the 877-lb. bell broke and the bell fell from its platform.

The support was subsequently repaired, and the bell was returned to its post. It stands ready to sound out the good news of another Bulldog win – but freshmen still aren't required to ring it as they were in the good old days.

It's a brutal truth that time just never stands still. The current of your life sweeps you along until you realize one day you've lived long enough to have a past. Part of it you cling to fondly. The stunts you pulled with your high-school buddies. Your first apartment. That dance with your first love. That special vacation. Those "good old days."

You hold on relentlessly to the memory of those old, familiar ways because of the stability they provide in our uncertain world. They will always be there even as times change and you age.

Another constant exists in your life, too. God has been a part of every event in your life that created a memory because he was there. He's always there with you; the question is whether you ignore him or make him a part of your day.

A "good old day" is any day shared with God.

It's gonna be sad not having the track people there. When the team drives up . . . and you see all of them, . . . you get both chills and a warm feeling at the same time.

-- Scott Woerner

Today is one of the "good old days"
if you share it with God.

STRANGE BUT TRUE

Read 1 Corinthians 1:18-31.

"The message of the cross is foolishness to those who are perishing, but to us who are being saved it is the power of God" (v. 18).

Is the strangest play in college football history the finish to the 1982 Stanford-Cal game when the Stanford band rushed onto the field and California scored? Maybe not. Consider the 1904 Georgia-Georgia Tech game.

The two teams played at the baseball field in Piedmont Park on "a miserably wet day." Late in the first half the Dogs made a magnificent goal-line stand and then lined up to punt. Punter Arthur Sullivan stood between the goal posts, which were on the goal line then, and a high fence. To his dismay, his punt struck the goal posts and bounced over the wall.

For several minutes, the players stood around, open-mouthed, wondering what to do next until the referee finally decided that since there were no end zones, the ball was still in play. Legendary sportswriter Grantland Rice recorded the strange scene that followed. "Suddenly both elevens made a dash at the slippery fence, sixteen feet high. To climb the rain-washed wall in itself was a Herculean task, but no sooner would a begrimed athlete scramble to the top than he would be yanked back by some rival."

Finally, Sullivan and a Tech player successfully topped the

fence with the referee right behind. On the other side, the ball was nowhere in sight, and only after a search of several minutes did the Techster find the ball buried in some deep grass. He fell on it and the ref signaled touchdown to complete the strangest play in Georgia football history. Only when the Tech player finally reappeared over the wall clutching the ball did the crowd finally know what had happened.

Life is just strange, isn't it? How else to explain the college bowl situation, Dr. Phil, tattoos, curling, tofu, and teenagers? Isn't it strange that today we have more ways to stay in touch with each other yet are losing the intimacy of personal contact?

And how strange is it that God let himself be killed by being nailed to a couple of pieces of wood? Think about that: the creator and ruler of the entire universe suffering the indignity and the torture that he did. And he did it quite willingly; this was God, after all. It's not like he wasn't capable of changing the course of events -- but he didn't. Isn't that strange?

But there's more that's downright bewildering. The cross, a symbol of disgrace, defeat, and death, ultimately became a worldwide symbol of hope, victory, and life. That's really strange.

So is the fact that love drove God to that cross. It's strange – but it's true.

It may sound strange, but many champions are made champions by setbacks.

-- Olympic champion Bob Richards

It's strange but true: God allowed himself to be killed on a cross because of his great love for you.

DECISIONS, DECISIONS

Read John 6:60-69.

"The words I have spoken to you are spirit and they are life. Yet there are some of you who do not believe" (vv. 63b-64a).

After the end of the 1981 basketball season, Dominique Wilkins had a decision to make.

As a sophomore he had averaged 23.6 points per game to win the SEC scoring title and had scored 732 points, both school records. The NBA came wooing. The Detroit Pistons pursued Wilkins hard, offering him a $400,000 salary, the second highest in NBA history. This was "a mountain of cash to a guy two years removed from . . . [a] housing project." Wilkins admitted he didn't know what he would have done "if Detroit had brought all that money into my room and put it on a bed. As it was, the figures were just that, figures. You couldn't see the money or feel it."

Wilkins was torn. He talked it over night after night with his roommate, Lamar Heard. Heard said Dominique would say, "I need the money" one time and then turn around and say, "I want to stay with you fellas."

Wilkins had until midnight on April 25, 1981, to notify the NBA of his intentions. At 5 p.m., he was still undecided. Even Coach Hugh Durham didn't know what Wilkins would do. In fact, Wilkins had surprised Durham earlier in the day by leaving town. It turned out he had driven to Atlanta for a final talk with his family.

At a 6:15 p.m. press conference, Wilkins announced, "Today, I committed to staying at Georgia."

What had been the determining factor in this tough decision that caused jubilation among Dog fans? He loved being at Georgia too much to leave it yet.

As was the case with Dominique Wilkins as he considered whether to stay in Athens or go, the decisions you have made along the way have shaped your life at every pivotal moment. Some decisions you made suddenly and frivolously; some you made carefully and deliberately; some were forced upon you. Perhaps decisions made for frivolous reasons have determined how your life unfolds, and you may have discovered that some of those spur-of-the-moment decisions have turned out better than your carefully considered ones.

Of all your life's decisions, however, none is more important than one you cannot ignore: What have you done with Jesus? Even in his time, people chose to follow Jesus or to reject him, and nothing has changed; the decision must still be made and nobody can make it for you. Carefully considered or spontaneous – how you arrive at a decision for Jesus doesn't matter; all that matters is that you get there.

If you make a decision that you think is the proper one at the time, then that's the correct decision.

-- Basketball Coach John Wooden

A decision for Jesus may be spontaneous or considered; what counts is that you make it.

AN AMERICAN HERO

Read 1 Samuel 16:1-13.

"Do not consider his appearance or his height, for . . . the Lord does not look at the things man looks at. . . . The Lord looks at the heart" (v. 7).

He was a poor orphan boy who became a star lineman for Georgia in the 1930s and an American hero in World War II.

Howard "Smiley" Johnson came to Georgia from Clarkesville, Tenn., in 1936 as a 160-pound freshman fullback, but it was on the line as a guard that he starred and lettered for three seasons. He received his nickname "because of his unfailingly pleasant manner."

He went on to play two seasons for the Green Bay Packers before he joined the Marine Corps in 1941. He was at Pearl Harbor as an enlisted man when the Japanese struck on Dec. 7.

Johnson was not the stereotypical Marine; he didn't cuss, smoke, or drink, and he read the Bible every night. But he was a superb Marine, so impressive in his officer candidate training that the Commandant of the Marine Corps himself came to his commissioning ceremony to pin his lieutenant's bars on in March 1943.

In 1944, Johnson won the country's second-highest military award — the Silver Star — for bravery under fire. His citation said he "daringly directed the defense" of his platoon when it came under attack, "exposing himself to heavy fire and helping annihilate in hand-to-hand combat the Japanese" who threatened his men.

Eight months after that at Iwo Jima, he was killed by exploding shell fragments while he was personally supervising the defenses of his platoon. A Navy corpsman said the last thing Johnson did was to point to four other dying marines and give this order: "Take care of my men first." He received a Gold Star for his actions.

A hero is commonly thought of as someone like Smiley Johnson who performs brave and dangerous feats that save or protect someone's life. You figure that excludes you.

But ask your son about that when you show him how to bait a hook, or your daughter when you show up for her dance recital. Look into the eyes of those Little Leaguers you help coach.

Ask God about heroism when you're steady in your faith. For God, a hero is a person with the heart of a servant. And if a hero is a servant who acts to save other's lives and to protect them from harm, then the greatest hero of all is Jesus Christ.

God seeks heroes today, those who will proclaim the name of their hero – Jesus – proudly and boldly, no matter how others may scoff or ridicule. God knows heroes when he sees them -- by what's in their hearts.

Heroes and cowards feel exactly the same fear; heroes just act differently.
-- Boxing trainer Cus D'Amato

God's heroes are those who remain steady in their faith while serving others.

BOLT OUT OF THE BLUE

Read Job 37.

> *"Listen! Listen to the roar of his voice. . . . He unleashes his lightning beneath the whole heaven and sends it to the ends of the earth" (vv. 2-3).*

Tennessee was ready for the Dogs. But they weren't ready for the bolt out of the blue that hit them right between the eyes -- and the thighs and everywhere else. They weren't ready for Herschel.

Freshman running back Herschel Walker didn't start in Georgia's 1980 season opener against Tennessee in Knoxville. But as the game progressed, nothing went right for Georgia, and in the second quarter Coach Vince Dooley decided to give Herschel a try. He told offensive coordinator George Haffner, "I'm putting Herschel in. Don't be afraid to let him carry the ball."

Herschel didn't do much early on, and Tennessee led comfortably 15-2 late in the third quarter. That's when the lightning bolt hit, and Herschel ran to Bulldog immortality. From the UT 16, quarterback Buck Belue pitched to Herschel. He found a hole and burst through. Near the goal line he met Tennessee safety Bill Bates, who would go on to have an excellent pro career. On this night, though, it was no contest. Herschel, "with a full head of steam, his powerful thighs churning, [ran] completely over Bates, chewing him up and spitting him out and leaving him stretched out on the Tartan turf." Touchdown Georgia.

Then with 11:16 left in the game, Herschel took another pitch and went nine yards for his second touchdown. Georgia won 16-15.

Nobody expected what hit Tennessee that night, not even the Georgia coaches. "I don't think anybody on our staff had any inkling of what was to come" when Herschel went into the game, Haffner said.

The unexpected is "a bolt out of the blue." Good – Herschel Walker's dazzling debut in Knoxville -- or bad -- a letter from the IRS. "A bolt out of the blue" speaks of the unpredictability of life, the power of a lightning bolt, and the workings of a divine presence.

The thunderbolt is often associated with God. Your insurance company classifies a lightning strike as "an act of God," conceding God's command of the thunderbolt.

This image of God – with a roar in his voice sending the lightning to all the earth – is one we often overlook. We prefer the gentle God of the April shower, the one who created bunnies and babies. But God is also lord of the hurricane and the creator of mountain lions and cobras.

God has all the power of the universe – from the atom to the lightning bolt -- at his disposal, and yet, he restrains it, acting toward you with gentleness and love.

There's one word that describes baseball -- 'You never know.'

-- Yogi Berra

The awesome power of lightning pales beside God's power to control it, and yet God acts toward you with gentleness and love.

DAY 60

CHANCE MEETING

Read Luke 24:13-35.

"That same day two of them were going to a village. . . . They were talking with each other about everything that had happened. . . . Jesus himself came up and walked along with them" (vv. 13-15).

He was in his back yard minding his own business when a chance meeting changed his life and UGA history.

Forrest G. "Spec" Towns was always a jumper. Growing up, he spent his summers on his grandparents' farm in Coffee County where, he said, "I never went through a gate. I would always jump over it." Despite his talent, he didn't run track in high school because his family couldn't afford the shoes. "My dad was doing well to provide me with a regular pair of shoes," Towns said.

One afternoon as he frequently did just for fun, Towns was in his backyard practicing high-jumping over a crossbar. Only this afternoon, his neighbor, a sports editor saw him. The writer was impressed enough by what he saw to write a column about Towns. Georgia track coach Weems Baskin read the column and signed Towns to a scholarship. The rest is Bulldog legend.

Towns was the 1936 Olympic champion in the 110-meter high hurdles and held world records in the 110-meter hurdles, the 120-yard high hurdles, and the 60- and 50-yard indoor hurdles. Vince Dooley said one of his greatest thrills was visiting the Berlin stadium in 1970 and seeing Towns' name inscribed on a huge plaque.

In 1939 Towns began a 34-year tenure as UGA track coach that included 21 SEC outdoor championships and five SEC indoor titles. In 1990, the Georgia track was named for him. Mel Rosen, coach of the 1992 U.S. men's Olympic track team, called Towns "the greatest track athlete Georgia ever had."

And it all started with a chance meeting out in the yard.

Maybe you met your spouse on a blind date or in Kroger's frozen food section. Perhaps a conversation in an elevator or over lunch led to a job offer.

Chance meetings often shape our lives. Some meetings, however, are too important to be left to what seems like the whims of life. If your child is sick, you don't wait until you happen to bump into a physician at Starbuck's to seek help.

So it is with Jesus. Too much is at stake to leave a meeting with him to chance. Instead, you intentionally seek him at church, in the pages of your Bible, on your knees in prayer, or through a conversation with a friend or neighbor. How you conduct the search doesn't matter; what matters is that you find him.

Once you've met him, the acquaintance should then be intentionally cultivated until it is a deep, abiding, life-shaping and life-changing friendship.

If you think it's hard to meet new people, try picking up the wrong golf ball.

-- Jack Lemmon

A meeting with Jesus should not be a chance encounter, but instead should be sought out.

LIMITED-TIME OFFER

Read Psalm 103.

"As for man, his days are like grass, he flourishes like a flower of the field; the wind blows over it and it is gone. . . . But from everlasting to everlasting the Lord's love is with those who fear him" (vv. 15-17).

There will be no more football at the university."

With that proclamation, the Georgia Athletic Association apparently sounded the death knell of football at the University of Georgia. A bill that outlawed football in all state-supported schools swept through both houses of the Georgia General Assembly.

The most tragic day in the history of Georgia football was the cause of the outrage that threatened the existence of the game in 1897. Against Virginia, Georgia's fullback, Richard Vonalbade Gammon, suffered a concussion while making a tackle. Doctors at the game realized he was in danger, and an ambulance took him to Grady Hospital. Gammon died before sunrise. Athens "was plunged into a deep gloom that spread to all areas of the state." Georgia Tech and Mercer disbanded their football teams.

Dr. Charles Herty, the Father of Georgia Football, was among the few who defended football after the tragedy. He wrote an open letter calling for better training and conditioning rather than football's abolition.

Among those who saw Herty's letter was Gammon's mother,

who promptly wrote a letter to her state representative that saved football in the South. She wrote, "It would be inexpressibly sad to have the cause he held so dear injured by his sacrifice. Grant me the right to request that my boy's death should not be used to defeat the most cherished object of his life."

Georgia's governor deferred to a mother's plea and never signed the bill abolishing football in the state.

A heart attack, cancer, or an accident will probably take -- or has already taken -- someone you know or love who is "too young to die" such as Von Gammon.

The death of a younger person never seems to "make sense." That's because such a death belies the common view of death as the natural end of a life lived well and lived long. Moreover, you can't see the whole picture as God does, so you can't know how the death furthers God's kingdom.

At such a time, you can seize the comforting truth that God is in control and therefore everything will be all right one day. You can also gain a sense of urgency in your own life by appreciating that God's offer of life through Jesus Christ is a limited-time offer that expires at your death – and there's no guarantee about when that will be.

No one knows when he or she is going to die, so if we're going to accept Christ, we'd better not wait because death can come in the blink of an eye.
--Bobby Bowden

God offers you eternal life through Jesus Christ, but you must accept it before your death when the offer expires.

PROMISES, PROMISES

Read 2 Corinthians 1:16-20.

"No matter how many promises God has made, they are 'Yes' in Christ" (v. 20).

Charley Trippi wouldn't give the college scouts the time of day – because he had made a promise.

The All-American halfback named in 2007 by ABC/ESPN as the 20th greatest player in college football history had a hardscrabble raising in Pennsylvania. For instance, the family had no money to buy him football shoes. "You got no business playing football," his father said. "You'll get your leg broke. And when you do, I'll break the other one."

But the local high school coach spied Trippi booming punts in his street shoes, and Trippi got his football footwear. He was the punter until a low snap forced him to chase the bounding ball. He "zigzagged his way for an 80-yard touchdown, which put him in the backfield to stay."

His junior year Trippi met Harold "War Eagle" Ketron, captain of the 1903 Georgia team, who gave the youngster a part-time job and later sent him to La Salle Academy on Long Island. After Trippi's sensational prep career, the scouts started coming around. He told them all he was not interested because "I had given my word to Mr. Ketron that I would sign with Georgia."

Trippi kept another promise about Georgia. After a sophomore season in which he teamed with Frank Sinkwich to lead Georgia to a win in the Rose Bowl and a national championship, he marched off to war. When he was discharged in 1945, he could have played professional football, but he returned to Athens because "I had promised coach [Wally] Butts. . . . I never regretted the decision."

The promises you make don't say much about you while the promises you keep tell everything.

The promise to your daughter to be there for her softball game. To your son to help him with his math homework. To your parents to come see them soon. To your spouse to remain faithful until death parts you. And remember what you promised God?

You may carelessly throw promises around, but you can never outpromise God, who is downright profligate with his promises. For instance, he has promised to love you always, to forgive you no matter what you do, and to prepare a place for you with him in heaven.

And there's more good news in that God operates on this simple premise: Promises made are promises kept. You can rely absolutely on God's promises.

The people to whom you make them should be able to rely just as surely on your promises.

In the everyday pressures of life, I have learned that God's promises are true.

-- Major leaguer Garret Anderson

God keeps his promises just as those who rely on you expect you to keep yours.

DOWNRIGHT CRAZY

Read Luke 13:31-35.

"Some Pharisees came to Jesus and said to him, 'Leave this place and go somewhere else. Herod wants to kill you.' He replied, 'Go tell that fox . . . I must keep going today and tomorrow and the next day'" (vv. 31-33).

A coach is supposed to sweet-talk recruits. You'd have to be crazy to just flat-out insult one. But that's what a coach did to Saudia Roundtree – and it saved Roundtree's career.

One of Georgia's greatest players, Roundtree was All-America and the Naismith College Player of the Year in 1996 as she led the Lady Dogs to the national championship game. In 1997, she received the Espy Award as the Best Female College Basketball Player in the country. She went on play professionally and was an American Basketball League All-Star.

But all of that was ahead of her when her spotty academics kept her from meeting Georgia's entrance requirements. This was after Coach Andy Landers had recruited her for years. He first saw her when she was an eighth grader and he was recruiting Stacey Ford, who came to Georgia. Devastated, Roundtree considered going to work and forgetting about college basketball, declaring, "That's it. I won't go anywhere."

But Landers intervened and hooked Roundtree up with Evelyn Blaylock, the coach at Kilgore (Texas) College. Accustomed to playing with boys and being coached by men, Roundtree was skeptical. She suggested Blaylock didn't have much to offer her. That's when the coach responded with a deliberate insult. She countered that perhaps Roundtree had even less to offer Kilgore. Miffed, Roundtree told Blaylock to send the papers.

Kilgore won the junior college national championship in 1993, and the next season Roundtree was named the Junior College Player of the Year. She was on her way to Georgia and a brilliant career.

Because a coach did something that seems downright crazy.

What some see as crazy often is shrewd instead. Like the time you went into business for yourself or when you decided to go back to school. Maybe it was when you fixed up that old house. Or when you bought that new company's stock.

You know a good thing when you see it but are also shrewd enough to spot something that's downright crazy. Jesus was that way too. He knew that entering Jerusalem was in complete defiance of all apparent reason and logic since a whole bunch of folks who wanted to kill him were waiting for him there.

Nevertheless, he went because he also knew that when the great drama had played out he would defeat not only his personal enemies but the most fearsome enemy of all: death itself.

It was, after all, a shrewd move that provided the way to your salvation.

Football is easy if you're crazy.

-- Bo Jackson

It's so good it sounds crazy -- but it's not: through faith in Jesus, you can have eternal life with God.

A SURE THING

Read Romans 8:28-30.

"We know that in all things God works for the good of those who love him, who have been called according to his purpose" (v. 28).

Vince Dooley called him "the greatest defensive player I ever coached," and yet out of high school, no college – including Georgia -- really wanted him.

Terry Hoage was not a sure thing. While Georgia fans everywhere in 1980 anxiously waited for Herschel Walker to make a decision, nobody was wondering about an unknown player from Huntsville, Texas, whom nobody was recruiting. Even the Georgia coaches couldn't decide whether they wanted to offer him the last scholarship they had left.

Hoage lacked speed and had missed his senior season with a leg injury, so any evaluation of his ability was uncertain. Coaches Bill Lewis and Steve Greer took a late recruiting swing to Texas and came back with little except that Hoage had a good attitude. "I was not sold on him as a player," Dooley said, but because Hoage was such a good student, the coaches decided to take a chance. "In fact," Dooley said, Hoage "had to work at football, but the classroom was a snap."

What they got was a player who made an immediate impact, blocking a Notre Dame field goal early in the national championship game in the Sugar Bowl. As Dooley put it, "When it came to the big play, no defensive player we ever had could match Hoage's overall ability and performance."

Hoage was an All-American defensive back in 1982 and 1983 and a two-time Academic All-America. He played 13 years in the NFL, and in 2000, this slow guy from Texas whom nobody really wanted because he wasn't a sure thing was inducted into the College Football Hall of Fame.

Statistics on paper don't really measure a player, and football games aren't played on paper. That is, you don't know about a player until he plays; you don't know who will win until the game is played.

Life doesn't get played on paper either, which means that living, too, comes laden with uncertainty. You never know what's going to happen tomorrow or even an hour from now. Oh, sure, you think you know. For instance, right now you may be certain that you'll be at work Monday morning or that you'll have a job next month. Life's uncertainties, though, can intervene at any time and disrupt your nice, pat expectations.

Ironically, while you can't know for sure about this afternoon, you can know for certain about forever. Eternity is a sure thing because it's in God's hands. Your unwavering faith and God's sure promises lock in a certain future for you.

You can never be certain in recruiting. It is not an exact science.
– Vince Dooley

Life is unpredictable and tomorrow is uncertain;
only eternity is a sure thing
-- because God controls it.

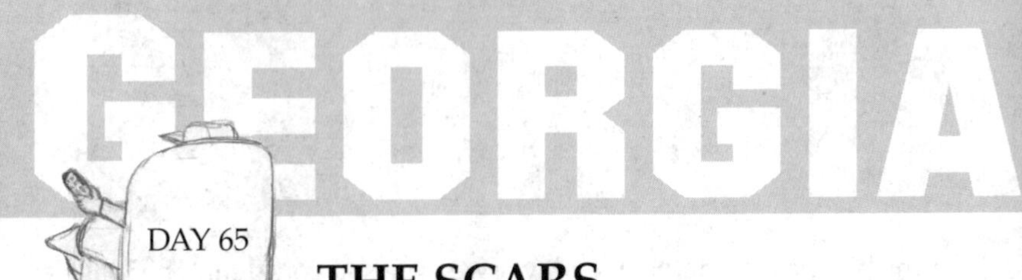

THE SCARS

Read John 20:19-31.

"Put your finger here; see my hands. Reach out your hand and put it into my side. Stop doubting and believe" (v. 27).

Bill Stanfill bears the scars of the game he loved.

Vince Dooley once called Stanfill "one of the greatest linemen to ever play the game." Dooley said the Cairo native was "everything you'd want" in a defensive lineman. "He combined speed, size, range, quickness and competitiveness."

Stanfill played defensive tackle for the Dogs in 1966, '67, and '68 and made All-SEC every season. In 1968, he made All-America, was named the SEC Lineman of the Year, and won the Outland Trophy as the nation's best lineman. He was selected to the 50th Anniversary All-SEC team in 1982.

He went on to become an All-Pro defensive end for the Miami Dolphins and was a star on the legendary 17-0 team of 1972. He is a member of the College Football Hall of Fame and the Georgia Sports Hall of Fame.

Football was very good to Bill Stanfill -- but it also exacted a price.

Knee and neck injuries brought an end to his playing career. He suffered four fused discs in his neck -- a problem that began when he jammed his neck in an exhibition game in 1975 -- and a bad disc in his lower back. He was in such pain that he couldn't tip his head back, had little use of his left thumb, and had considerable loss of hand and arm strength. He needed three surgeries to correct the problems. He had both hips replaced in 2001. Finally, in 2003, he was pain free for the first time in a long time.

Stanfill admitted he "had to give up a lot to play football." But "you know what?" he said. "If I were 18 years old right now, I would be glad to do it all over again. That's how much I loved going to Georgia."

You've got scars too, even if they're not from a football career. That car wreck left a good one. So did that bicycle crash. Maybe we better not talk about that time you said, "Hey, watch this!" Your scars are part of your life story, the residue of the pain you've encountered. People's scars are so unique and ubiquitous they're used to identify bodies.

Even Jesus proved who he was by the scars of the nail marks in his hands and his side. How interesting it is that even after his resurrection, Jesus bore the scars of the pain he endured. Apparently, he bears them still even as he sits upon his throne in Heaven.

Why would he even have them in the first place? Why would the almighty God of the universe submit to treatment that left him wounded and scarred?

He did it for you. Jesus' scars tell the story of his love for you.

Andre Dawson has a bruised knee and is listed as day-to-day. Aren't we all?

-- Announcer Vin Scully

In your scars lie stories. The same is true for Jesus, whose scars tell of his love for you.

DAY 66

THE PRIZE

Read Philippians 3:10-16.

"I press on toward the goal to win the prize for which God has called me heavenward in Christ Jesus" (v. 14).

As a senior, Jay McAuley rarely left the bench, and yet his teammates and coach respected him so much they selected him to the most esteemed position in athletics: team captain.

McAuley was one of the most uncommon of college athletes. In October 2002, he walked on to the Georgia basketball team and stayed with the team for four years, a rarity. He had some offers from small colleges out of high school, but decided to come to Georgia "on the HOPE scholarship and see where the chips would fall." He got a little mop-up duty in three games his freshman year before the roof caved in on the basketball program and Dennis Felton was summoned to set everything aright.

Suddenly, Jay McAuley became walk-on extraordinaire. Roster shortages and injuries forced Felton to play him in 35 games over the next two seasons, including back-to-back starts and all 40 minutes against Clemson.

McAuley was a leader in the dressing room. Freshman Terrance Woodbury said of him, "His word is big around here. He speaks up a lot. He says what he thinks when he feels like it. . . . He definitely has our respect."

In 2005-06, with better players on the squad, senior McAuley didn't get to play much, but he was not disappointed. That meant the program was headed in the right direction. To honor this rare walk-on, the team named him one of its captains, recognition Jay McAuley never sought. "It's a great honor, and I'm flattered by it," McAuley said. "I'm just proud to be part of the team. . . . I just love Georgia basketball."

Even the most modest and self-effacing among us – like Jay McAuley -- can't help but be pleased by prizes and honors. They symbolize the approval and appreciation of others, whether it's being named the team captain, an Employee of the Month trophy, a plaque for sales achievement, or the sign declaring yours as the neighborhood's prettiest yard.

Such prizes and awards are often the culmination of the pursuit of personal achievement and accomplishment. They represent accolades and recognition from the world. Nothing is inherently wrong with any of that as long as we keep them in perspective.

That is, we must never let such awards become idols that we worship or lower our sight from the greatest prize of all and the only one truly worth winning. It's one that won't rust, collect dust, or leave us wondering why we worked so hard to win it in the first place. The ultimate prize is eternal life, and it's ours through Jesus Christ.

A gold medal is a wonderful thing, but if you're not enough without it, you'll never be enough with it.

-- *John Candy in* Cool Running

The greatest prize of all doesn't require competition to claim it; God has it ready to hand to you through Jesus Christ.

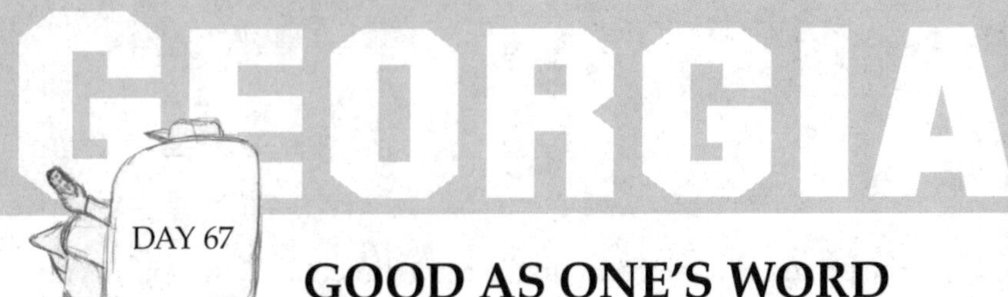

DAY 67

GOOD AS ONE'S WORD

Read Matthew 12:33-37.

"For out of the overflow of the heart the mouth speaks. The good man brings good things out of the good stored up in him, and the evil man brings evil things out of the evil stored up in him" (vv. 34-35).

Someone said he "might just be the most popular figure in the history of Georgia sports." And he was never in for one play in any sport for Georgia.

He is Larry Munson, who was the voice of the Dogs for more than forty years.

While Munson "has achieved an exalted status in the lore of Georgia football," there was a time when he wasn't very popular among the Bulldog Nation; at the very least, Georgia fans "were slow to embrace Munson the outsider." He was a Yankee from Minnesota, and he didn't move to Georgia after he landed the Bulldog job in 1966. Even Vince Dooley noticed this, saying, "He wasn't part of the team and the program. He lived in Nashville; he was here only one day a week." Perhaps most incredible of all, Munson's delivery didn't excite any one. He was like a professional announcer, "totally impartial, cold, dry."

That all changed in November 1973. When the Dogs pulled out a last-minute 35-31 win over Tennessee in Neyland Stadium, Munson blurted out, "WE'VE just beaten Tennessee!" From then on, he cast aside any pretensions of objectivity, enduring the agonies of the doomed with every Georgia fumble or dropped pass and going completely bonkers over the touchdowns and the wins -- just as his listeners did. The result was an unconventional broadcasting technique and a love affair with Bulldog fans that lasted for decades until fading health finally forced his retirement. Even after television moved in, Georgia fans routinely turned off the sound on their set and hung on Munson's every word.

These days, everybody's got something to say and likely as not a place to say it. Talk radio, 24-hour sports and news TV channels, *Oprah, The View*. Talk has really become cheap.

But words still have power, and that includes not just those of the talking heads, hucksters, and pundits on television, but ours also. Our words are perhaps the most powerful force we possess for good or for bad. The words we speak today can belittle, wound, humiliate, and destroy. They can also inspire, heal, protect, and create. Our words both shape and define us. They also reveal to the world the depth of our faith.

We should never make the mistake of underestimating the power of the spoken word. After all, speaking the Word was the only means Jesus had to get his message across – and look what he managed to do.

We must always watch what we say, because others sure will.

Be a man of your word, [my father] always taught me. Do what you say you are going to do.

-- Vince Dooley

Choose your words carefully; they are the most powerful force you have for good or for bad.

HUMBLE PIE

Read Matthew 23:1-12.

"The greatest among you will be your servant. For whoever exalts himself will be humbled, and whoever humbles himself will be exalted" (vv. 11-12).

Vince Dooley once got a double lesson in humility.

Dan Magill told the story at a charity roast of Coach Dooley that back in the summer of 1964 -- prior to Dooley's first football season in Athens -- he asked Magill, the tennis coach, if there were anybody who could give him a good tennis workout. Magill produced Howard Shelton, who was rather senior. Dooley took Magill aside and asked, "Haven't you got someone younger?" Magill replied, "I'm sorry, he's the only player available, but he'll give you a good workout." Magill might have had a smile up his sleeve because Shelton was the state 70-year-old champion. Dooley didn't win a game off him.

As Magill put it, "I could detect that Coach Dooley was mad about being humiliated by this old man." When Magill saw Dooley again, he said he wanted to play somebody younger. This time Magill rounded up a 12-year-old who was quite small for his age. Again, Dooley was exasperated. "Is this little boy the only player here?" he asked. Magill's answer was the same as before: "He'll give you a good workout."

Again, he must have grinned as the new football coach went to the courts and was blitzed 6-0, 6-0. The boy was Danny Birchmore, the reigning 12-and-under state champion. He would win the U.S. Boys' 18 clay court title, beating Jimmy Connors, and would be a two-time All-America at Georgia.

After that, Magill said, Dooley claimed "football knee" in not playing tennis again.

Life usually finds a way to teach us not to think too highly of ourselves. We get fired from a job. We fail to make a sports team or a cheerleading squad. There's always somebody younger, smarter, better looking, and more aggressive around.

But Jesus said that humility is to be a way of life, and he demonstrated what he meant by the way he lived. Humility doesn't demand abject poverty, ongoing afflictions, or a complete lack of social status. Humility, rather, is an attitude toward God and other people.

God calls us in Jesus to be willing servants, always looking for the chance to help others. We banish both thoughts and acts of violence, arrogance, and selfish pride toward others, replacing them with a lifestyle that values peace and harmony.

Society certainly does not think or function in this way. Moreover, in Jesus' topsy-turvy kingdom, today's servants are tomorrow's exalted.

Mental toughness is humility because it behooves all of us to remember that simplicity is the sign of greatness and meekness is the sign of true strength.

– Vince Lombardi

To be humbled today in the name of Jesus is to be exalted forever in the presence of Jesus.

DAY 69

THE BAD TIMES

Read Philippians 1:3-14.

"What has happened to me has really served to advance the gospel. . . . Most of the brothers in the Lord have been encouraged to speak the word of God more courageously and fearlessly" (vv. 12, 14).

Matt Stinchcomb went through some bad times at Georgia.

He personally was very successful at UGA. He was an All-American tackle in both 1997 and 1998 and a two-time Academic All-America. He won the Draddy Award as college football's top scholar. But even Stinchcomb admitted, "I went through one of the strangest times in the history of Georgia football."

Those strange times included three different coaches in about three weeks his freshman year. After the 1995 team went 6-6, Ray Goff was replaced by Glen Mason, who decided a week after accepting the Georgia job to stay at Kansas. Jim Donnan and a new staff then came in, which Stinchcomb called "a tough transition" because not a single one of the former coaches was retained.

"The first season [1996] was tough," he said as the Dogs went 5-6 and were "a beleaguered football team." Georgia won ten games in 1997 and whipped Florida 37-17, but the team played itself out of a major bowl by losing to Auburn. The 1998 squad got off to a 4-0 start but finished weakly with losses to Florida and Georgia Tech. Speaking of the Tech game, Stinchcomb summarized his whole time in Athens when he said, "A lot of strange things happened in that game – and they all went against us."

What did Stinchcomb think about his years at Georgia, which included their shares of disappointment? "I wouldn't trade anything" for them, he said. "I was lucky to be a part of [Georgia football]." Matt Stinchcomb experienced some bad times, but he remains a good witness for UGA football.

Loved ones die. You're downsized. Your biopsy looks cancerous. Your spouse could be having an affair. Hard, tragic times are as much a part of life as breath.

This applies to Christians too. Faith in Jesus Christ does not exempt anyone from pain. Jesus promises he will be there for us to lead us through the valleys; he never promises that we will not enter them.

The question therefore becomes how you handle the bad times. You can buckle to your knees in despair and cry, "Why me?" Or you can hit your knees in prayer and ask, "What do I do with this?"

Setbacks and tragedies are opportunities to reveal and to develop true character and abiding faith. Your faithfulness -- not your skipping merrily along through life without pain -- is what reveals the depth of your love for God.

If I were to say, "God, why me?" about the bad things, then I should have said, "God, why me?" about the good things that happened in my life.

– Arthur Ashe

Faithfulness to God requires faith even in -- especially in -- the bad times.

DRY RUN

Read 1 Kings 16:29-17:1, 18:1.

"Elijah the Tishbite, from Tishbe in Gilead, said to Ahab, 'As the Lord, the God of Israel, lives, whom I serve, there will be neither dew nor rain in the next few years except at my word'" (v. 17:1).

The drought was of Biblical proportions. It lasted eight years.

From 1949 to 1956, Georgia Tech beat Georgia eight straight times. The drought was finally broken in 1957 when All-SEC fullback Theron Sapp almost single-handedly defeated Tech 7-0.

Sapp signed a scholarship with Georgia in 1954, but he broke his neck shortly thereafter in a diving accident. Doctors said he would never play football again. A dejected coach Wally Butts told Sapp he could keep his scholarship and help the team as its manager; Sapp, however, was determined to play again. He spent his freshman year at Georgia in a body cast and played on the B-team his sophomore season.

Sapp claimed the starting fullback job as a junior and achieved Bulldog immortality on Nov. 30. On the bus ride from Athens to Grant Field that day, Sapp told "Coach Butts that we were going to win the game. I told him I didn't sleep a wink last night, that all I could think about was that we were going to break the drought."

The game was scoreless in the third quarter when Sapp recovered a Tech fumble at midfield. He carried nine times on the subsequent drive. After quarterback Charlie Britt hit Jimmy Orr for 13 yards to the Tech 26, "from then on it was all Sapp . . . Sapp . . . Sapp." Six straight times, Sapp hit the Tech line, and then on fourth down from the one, he scored. The drought was over. The Man Who Broke the Drought "did as much for Georgia pride with one touchdown as anyone in Bulldogs history."

Sapp's #40 jersey was retired two months after the 16-3 win over Tech in 1958.

You can walk across that river you boated on in the spring. The city's put all neighborhoods on water restriction, and that beautiful lawn you fertilized and seeded will turn a sickly, pale green and may lapse all the way to brown. Somebody wrote "Wash Me" on the rear window of your truck.

The sun bakes everything, including the concrete. The earth itself seems exhausted, just barely hanging on. It's a drought.

It's the way a soul looks that shuts God out.

God instilled thirst in us to warn us of our body's need for physical water. He also gave us a spiritual thirst that can be quenched only by his presence in our lives. Without God, we are like tumbleweeds, dried out and windblown, offering the illusion of life where there is only death.

Living water – water of life – is readily available in Jesus. We may drink our fill, and thus we slake our thirst and end our soul's drought – forever.

Drink before you are thirsty. Rest before you are tired.
-- Paul de Vivie, father of French cycle touring

Our souls thirst for God's refreshing presence.

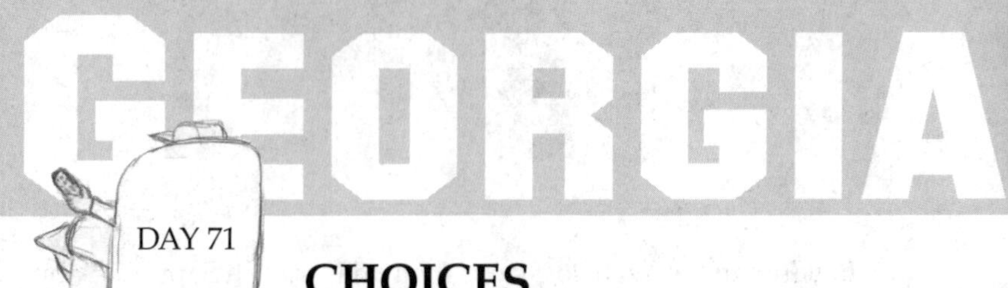

DAY 71

CHOICES

Read Deuteronomy 30:15-20.

"I have set before you life and death, blessings and curses. Now choose life, so that you and your children may live" (v. 19).

Herschel Walker had to choose: Georgia or Southern Cal.

Though he played his high school ball in the relatively unknown burg of Wrightsville, by his senior season Walker was anything but relatively unknown. One Wrightsville resident said, "People started lining up at 4:30 in the afternoon on game day" to see Walker play. And they weren't all just fans; many were suitors from practically every major college in the country with one aim: to convince Walker to choose their school.

Both football and basketball seasons came and went with no decision, but Walker had managed to narrow his list to Southern Cal and Georgia. Finally, on Easter morning 1980 – a full month after other prospects had announced their choices -- Herschel chose Southern California though his family wanted Georgia. "He liked Georgia. He liked the Georgia people. But he felt he was being pushed," and Herschel Walker liked to make up his own mind. He had only to awaken the coaches in California with a collect call to tell them of his choice.

But again Herschel hesitated. If he went to Southern Cal, his family would only rarely see him play. He never did know exactly what made him change his mind that day, but what was perhaps the most fateful decision in Georgia football history went something like this: "Standing in the kitchen, [Herschel] simply blurted it out: 'Okay,' he said. 'Call Coach [Gary] Phillips and tell him I'll sign with Georgia.'" One of Walker's high school coaches, Phillips was the first outside the family to know of the choice that made front-page news all over the state and had the entire Bulldog Nation celebrating.

As with Herschel Walker, your life is the sum of the choices you've made. That is, you have arrived at this moment and this place in your life because of the choices you made in your past. Your love of the Dawgs. Your spouse or the absence of one. Mechanic, teacher, or beautician. Condo in Buckhead or ranch home in Dublin. Dog, cat, or goldfish. You chose; you live with the results.

That includes the most important choice you ever will have to make: faith or the lack of it. That we have the ability to make decisions when faced with alternatives is a gift from God, who allows that faculty even when he's part of the choice. We can choose whether or not we will love him. God does remind us that this particular choice has rather extreme consequences: Choosing God's way is life; choosing against him is death.

Life or death. What choice is that?

The choices you make in life make you.

-- John Wooden

God gives you the freedom to choose: life or death; what kind of choice is that?

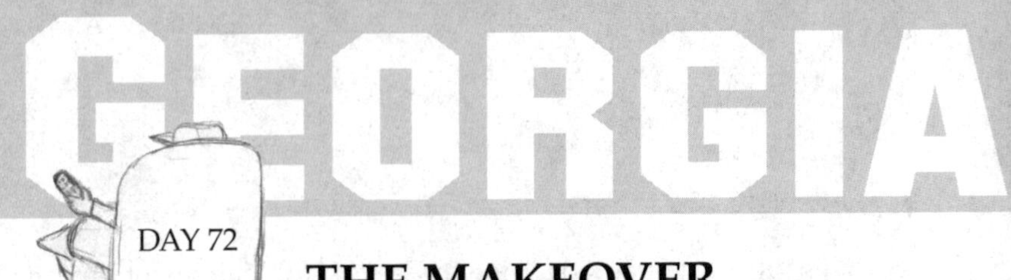

THE MAKEOVER

Read 2 Corinthians 5:11-21.

"If anyone is in Christ, he is a new creation; the old has gone, the new has come!" (v. 17)

Georgia's first basketball All-America was on loan from the football team.

Joe "Zippy" Morocco's first love was basketball, but in 1948 UGA didn't hand out roundball scholarships. Morocco thus played football and then made himself over into a basketball player when the season ended.

It wasn't easy. "Making the transition from one sport to another was challenging in many different ways," he said. "Physically, your body is 'tight' after a season of football. Your muscles are conditioned to one kind of activity, and then you go straight into another sport that uses a different set of muscles." Morocco also understood that he started basketball season late. "When you play football," he said, "you're playing catch-up for the first month that you're out there" on the basketball court.

Morocco was small, only 5'10" and less than 160 pounds, but he was fast, and Coach Wally Butts used him on kickoff and punt returns. His career average per punt return of 14.2 yards is still the Georgia record, and he averaged nearly ten yards every time he touched the football.

On the basketball court, though, is where Morocco excelled. Drafted by pro football's Philadelphia Eagles, Morocco decided to remain at Georgia because he had a year of basketball eligibility left. In 1953, playing basketball fulltime, Morocco blossomed. He scored more points than any player in SEC history, was named the conference's most valuable player (a first for Georgia), and was named All-America despite playing for a 7-18 team.

Georgia has had many athletes who made themselves over in moving from one sport to another, but Zippy Morocco remains among the best.

Ever considered a makeover? TV shows have shown us how changes in clothes, hair, and makeup and some weight loss can radically alter the way a person looks. But these changes are only skin deep. Even with a makeover, the real you — the person inside — remains unchanged. How can you make over that part of you?

By giving your heart and soul to Jesus -- just as you give up your hair to the makeover stylist. You won't look any different; you won't dance any better; you won't suddenly start talking smarter.

The change is on the inside where you are brand new because the model for all you think and feel is now Jesus. He is the one you care about pleasing. Made over by Jesus, you realize that gaining his good opinion — not the world's — is all that really matters. And he isn't interested in how you look but how you act.

Don't think that the way you are today is the way you'll always be.
-- Vince Dooley

Jesus is the ultimate makeover artist; he can make you over without changing the way you look.

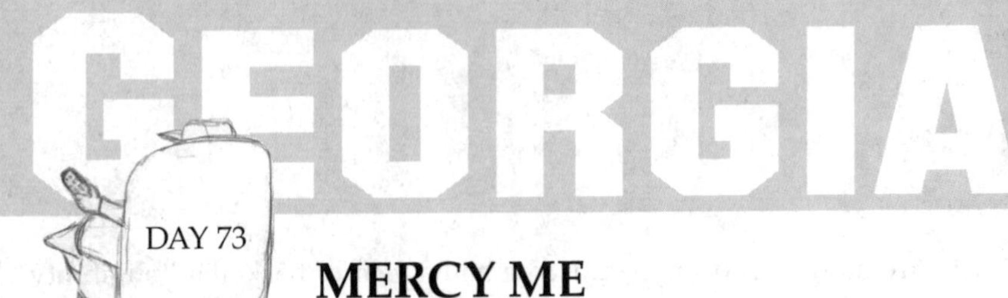

MERCY ME

Read Ephesians 2:1-10.

"Because of his great love for us, God, who is rich in mercy, made us alive with Christ even when we were dead in transgressions – it is by grace you have been saved" (vv. 4-5).

Tech didn't beg for mercy, but the Dogs gave it anyhow in 1975.

When Tech and Georgia met on national television on Thanksgiving night, most folks expected a close game. The Dogs came in 8-2 while Tech was 7-3, but Erk Russell's Junkyard Dogs made a play on the first play from scrimmage and the rout was on.

Bobby Thompson intercepted a pass and returned it to the Tech 12. Ray Goff scored from the two, and after only 2:11, Georgia led 7-0. Tech never recovered. Later in the half, Georgia went 97 yards in two plays. Goff went for 19 yards to the 22, and Glynn Harrison hit a hole behind All-American Randy Johnson and raced 78 yards for a touchdown. Only a few minutes later, end Lawrence Craft returned a Tech fumble 20 yards for another touchdown. Allan Leavitt was true again on the extra point. If Tech was looking for some relief, they didn't get it – yet. Al Pollard plowed in from the two after Bill Krug blocked a Jacket punt and Matt Robinson hit Richard Appleby for a 32-yard gain. Georgia led 28-0 at the half despite running only twelve plays.

The score went to 42-0 in the third quarter with a Goff-to-Mark Wilson touchdown pass and another Pollard TD run. The 42-0 score marked Georgia's first-ever 40-point lead over Tech. How bad could it get? 56-0? 63-0? Even 70-0? Being the Christian man he is, Vince Dooley showed mercy, pulling his starters and letting Tech save some face with a 42-26 final score. One writer tagged him "St. Vincent the Merciful."

A drunk slams into your car, hospitalizing you and your family. Your worthless son-in-law walks out on your daughter. Your boss passes you over for a promotion you deserve. Some addict burglarizes your house.

Somebody sometime in your life has hurt you. What's your attitude toward them? Do you scream for revenge and payback? Or do you extend mercy, showing compassion and kindness all out of proportion to what's been done to you?

Mercy is the appeal of last resort. When we are guilty, our only hope is mercy. Our only prayer is that the judge will not remorselessly hand down the sentence we deserve.

Of all God's attributes, none is more astounding than his penchant for mercy. Through Jesus, God provided the way to save us from the sentence we deserve. Through Jesus, God made his divine mercy available to us all. In so doing, though, God expects that we who avail ourselves of his mercy will show mercy toward others. We reap what we sow.

If you race merely for the tributes from others, you will be at the mercy of their expectations.

-- Professional triathlete Scott Tinley

**To sow mercy in our lifetime now
is to reap mercy from God
when we stand guiltily before him.**

THE BAD GUYS

Read Ephesians 6:10-18.

"Our struggle is not against flesh and blood, but against the rulers, against the authorities, against the powers of this dark world and against the spiritual forces of evil in the heavenly realms" (v. 12).

Some Georgia fans were making a routine trip home from a game -- and somebody tried to kill them.

In 1900, Georgia lost to Sewanee 21-6 at Atlanta's Piedmont Park. That evening the Georgia fans boarded a train for Athens, unaware four men had hatched a plan to wreck the train at the Yellow River trestle west of Lawrenceville. After the train had "plunged to its destruction the bandits would rob the baggage and mail cars" and the dead and injured passengers. They even brought an axe along in case any of the injured Bulldog fans offered any resistance. When the men heard the train drawing near, two of them walked onto the trestle and began to separate the rails with crowbars and wedges while two others kept watch.

But one of the desperados had boasted about their planned exploit, and the two ringleaders were caught in the act while the lookouts scurried quietly away into the bushes. Police officers warned the train with a lantern, and the express shuddered to a stop safely short of the bridge. When the handcuffed men were brought onto the train, word of their nefarious plan leaked to the passengers, who "were soon in an uproar. They rushed the captives and tried to wrench them from the officers, intending to take them off the train for the application of some immediate form of justice." But the tracks were repaired and the train resumed its journey before any real damage could be done to the cowering twosome. The men were jailed in Lawrenceville, and the passengers had an exciting story to tell.

Just like those train-riding Georgia fans, we never really know what evil is swirling around us. We do know that a just and good God tolerates the existence of evil even if why this is so remains part of the inscrutableness of God.

Evil is not intrinsically a part of God's physical world, which God declared to be "good." Rather, evil is a function of the spirit world, of Satan and his flunkies. Human beings are thus the focus of an ongoing cosmic struggle between good and evil. The primary battleground is our hearts, so we struggle with temptation even after we surrender our lives to Christ. The forces of evil don't concede defeat; they work harder.

The day of God's own choosing will come when all evil will be defeated and goodness will rule unopposed. Not only will the spiritual forces of evil be eradicated, but so will those humans who have sided with them.

Evil is for losers.

A boxing match is like a cowboy movie. People pay to see the bad guys get beat.

-- Former heavyweight champion Sonny Liston

Evil may win temporarily – even in your heart – but to follow Jesus is to live daily in the knowledge of good's ultimate triumph.

FAMILY MEN

Read Mark 3:31-35.

"He said, 'Here are my mother and my brothers! Whoever does God's will is my brother and sister and mother'" (vv. 34-35).

Twins Jonas and Jarvis Hayes are so close that in December 2001 in a game against Minnesota, Jonas got hurt and it was Jarvis who vomited.

"He's my brother, man," Jarvis explained after a visit to a trash can at halftime precipitated by his checking out Jonas' dislocated index finger. "When he hurts, I hurt. I couldn't think about anything else until I got into the locker room and saw him."

It was always about family for the Hayes twins. Out of high school, they insisted that any basketball scholarship offers be made to both of them. Only three schools -- Western Carolina, Mercer, and Jacksonville State – agreed to take them both, and they went to Western Carolina in 1999.

When the head coach was fired after the season, the boys' father, James, made a call to UGA and said simply, "I've got these two sons from Douglass High in Atlanta who are at Western Carolina and want to come home." And so two of the most popular players in Georgia basketball history came to Athens.

In 2002, Jarvis won the SEC's scoring title, averaging 18.6 points per game. He was Georgia's first two-time All-SEC player since Dominique Wilkins. In 2000, Jonas would have led the league in field-goal accuracy had he shot enough times to qualify.

They were excellent basketball players, but as their insistence on playing college ball together demonstrated, they were family men first. "You just instill things into your children," their proud father said. "Just be good people. Don't forget where all your blessings come from in the beginning and you will go far."

Some wit said families are like fudge, mostly sweet with a few nuts. You can probably call the names of your sweetest relatives, whom you cherish, and of the nutty ones too, whom you mostly try to avoid at a family reunion.

Like it or not, you have a family, and that's God's doing. God cherishes the family so much that he chose to live in one as a son, a brother, and a cousin.

One of Jesus' more startling actions was to redefine the family. No longer is it a single household of blood relatives or even a clan or a tribe. Jesus' family is the result not of an accident of birth but rather a conscious choice. All those who do God's will are members of Jesus' family.

What a startling and wonderful thought! You have family members out there you don't even know who stand ready to love you just because you're part of God's family.

Football has affected my entire family's lifestyle. My little boy can't go to bed unless we give him a two-minute warning.

-- Former NFL coach Dick Vermeil

For followers of Jesus, family comes not from a shared ancestry but from a shared faith.

ANSWERING THE CALL

Read 1 Samuel 3:1-18.

"The Lord came and stood there, calling as at the other times, 'Samuel! Samuel!' Then Samuel said, 'Speak, for your servant is listening'" (v. 10).

Dicky Clark's football career at Georgia was going nowhere – until he gave up a dream and answered his team's call.

As a sophomore in 1974, Clark started at quarterback until Matt Robinson took over after a loss to Mississippi State. Offensive coordinator Bill Pace told Clark, "We're going to let Matt play a little bit and see what happens." "What happened," Clark said, "was that Matt played the rest of the year. It looked like I was out of a job."

At the Tech game, Clark remembered that "at halftime my socks were literally frozen, so I took them off and asked the equipment manager for some fresh ones. He said, 'Only the guys who are playing get dry socks.'" Clark thought of quitting.

But he didn't, and in the spring of 1975, defensive coordinator Erk Russell approached him with a proposal. He wanted the benchwarming quarterback to move to defensive end, a good change for Clark and the best thing for the team. Clark agreed, though "it was tough giving up on being a quarterback; that's what I had always been. But . . . I wanted to play."

In the second game of the season, interestingly enough against Mississippi State, Clark intercepted a pass and scored. The Dogs won 28-6. He was named the SEC's Lineman of the Week, and in 1976 he was All-SEC and served as the defensive captain of the SEC champions.

Greatness in any team sport often requires that the players do what Dickey Clark did: answer the call by doing whatever is necessary to help the team even if it means putting aside personal dreams and goals.

A team player is someone who does whatever the coach calls upon him to do for the good of the team. Something quite similar occurs when God places a specific call upon a Christian's life.

This is much scarier, though, than shifting positions on a football team as Dickey Clark did. The way many folks understand it is that answering God's call means going into the ministry, packing the family up, and moving halfway around the world to some place where folks have never heard of air conditioning, fried chicken, paved roads, or the Georgia Bulldogs. Zambia. The Philippines. Cleveland even.

Not for you, no thank you. And who can blame you?

But God usually calls folks to serve him where they are. In fact, God put you where you are right now, and he has a purpose in placing you there.

Wherever you are, you are called to serve him.

It was like being in a foreign country.
-- Welsh soccer player Ian Rush on playing in Italy

God calls you to serve him right now right where you are.

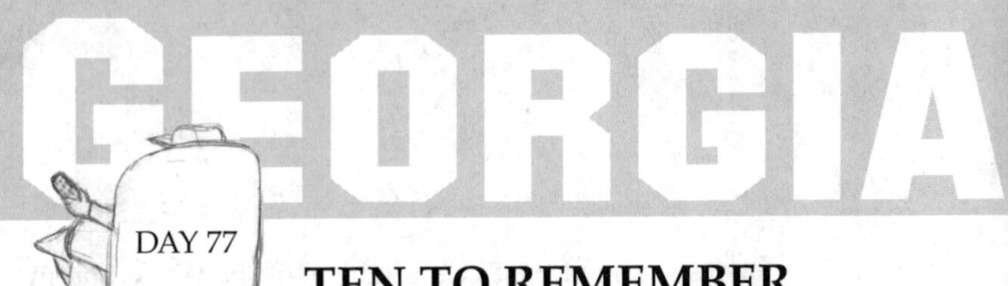

TEN TO REMEMBER

Read Exodus 20:1-17.

"God spoke all these words: 'I am the Lord your God . . . . You shall have no other gods before me'" (vv. 1, 3).

Prior to the final home meet of the 2009 season, her last as head coach of the Georgia gymnastics team, Suzanne Yoculan took a moment with sportswriter Peter Cox to remember and to list the top ten most memorable moments in her career.

At the top of her list was her first meet. In January 1984, Georgia hosted Alabama; two-hundred people showed up. "We have a lot of work to do to fill this arena," Yoculan thought.

2. The team's first championship: the Dogs were ranked fifth when they halted Utah's string of five straight titles. "We were so new," team member Lucy Wener recalled. "When we won, it was quite a surprise."

3. The 1989 NCAA championship, which Georgia hosted.

4. Georgia's first 10, which was scored by Wener, the Dogs' first Olympian, at the 1989 NCAA Championships.

5. The 1993 NCAA championship, which Georgia dominated.

6. A packed Stegeman Coliseum: On Jan. 28, 1994, more than 10,000 fans filled the place for a meet with LSU. Yoculan said she never thought she'd see the day when people were scalping tickets for a gymnastics meet.

7. Karin Lichey's perfect night: On Feb. 23, 1996, the freshman became the first and only gymnast in history to score a perfect

40.0 in an NCAA meet.

8. The 1997 NCAA Championship loss: Yoculan said this team was her best ever but three gymnasts fell off the beam.

9. Two straight NCAA championships in 1998 and 1999.

10. Opening the Suzanne Yoculan Gymnastics Center: In 2007, the team moved from "a small, shared, run-down building" into a pristine practice space with 16,000 square feet.

Like Suzanne Yoculan, you've made your list. You're ready to go now: a gallon of paint and a water hose from the hardware store; chips, peanuts, and sodas from the grocery store for watching tonight's football game with your buddies; the tickets for the band concert. Your list helps you remember.

God also made a list once of things he wanted you to remember; it's called the Ten Commandments. Just as your list reminds you to do something, so does God's list remind you of how you are to act in your dealings with other people and with him.

A life dedicated to Jesus is a life devoted to relationships, and God's list emphasizes that the social life and the spiritual life of the faithful cannot be sundered. God's relationship to you is one of unceasing, unqualified love, and you are to mirror that divine love in your relationships with others.

In case you forget, you have a list.

Society today treats the Ten Commandments as if they were the ten suggestions. Never compromise on right or wrong.
-- College baseball coach Gordie Gillespie

God's list is a set of instructions on how you are to conduct yourself with other people and with him.

DAY 78

TOP SECRET

Read Romans 2:1-16.

"This will take place on the day when God will judge men's secrets through Jesus Christ, as my gospel declares" (v. 16).

Joel Eaves had a secret -- one that would change the destiny not only of the UGA football program but all of UGA athletics.

Eaves was hired away from Auburn in 1963 as the Georgia athletic director. His mission was "to bring stability to a sports program that was in tatters." On Dec. 3, 1963, Eaves made the most important and probably the most courageous move of his career. He called an unknown 31-year-old freshman football coach whom he had coached with at Auburn and offered him the head football job in Athens. The next morning, Vince Dooley -- Eaves' great big secret -- was on a plane to Athens.

Not that much secrecy was required. "I could have walked through the middle of Athens and no one would have ever noticed me," Dooley said. Nevertheless, before sending Sports Information Director Dan Magill to pick Dooley up at the Athens airport, Eaves stressed the necessity for secrecy. So Magill instructed Dooley to lie down in the backseat as they neared the downtown Holiday Inn. Thus did the man who would change UGA's athletic history make his rather ignominious entrance into Athens.

Dooley was so unknown that UGA President O.C. Aderhold forgot his name at the Dec. 5 press conference announcing the hire. Jangling his keys as he struggled with his memory, he referred to Dooley several times as "our fine young coach."

With such anonymity, why was Eaves so concerned with secrecy? He had received unprecedented authority from his athletics board to make this crucial hire, and he wanted them to hear it from the source and not the newspapers.

As Joel Eaves was with the hiring of his new football coach, we have to be vigilant about the information we prefer to keep secret. Much information about us—from credit reports to what movies we rent—is readily available to prying and persistent persons. In our information age, people we don't know may know a lot about us—or at least they can find out. And some of them may use this information for harm.

While diligence may allow us to be reasonably successful in keeping some secrets from the world at large, we should never deceive ourselves into believing we are keeping secrets from God. God knows everything about us, including the things we wouldn't want proclaimed at church. All our sins, mistakes, failures, shortcomings, quirks, prejudices, and desires – God knows all our would-be secrets.

But here's something God hasn't keep a secret: No matter what he knows about us, he loves us still.

The secret to success is to start from scratch and keep on scratching.
-- former NFL coach Dennis Green

We have no secrets before God, and it's no secret that he nevertheless loves us still.

DAY 79

PRESSURE COOKER

Read 1 Kings 18:16-40.

"Answer me, O Lord, answer me, so these people will know that you, O Lord, are God" (v. 37).

Everybody's watching you. Your team's hopes for a national championship are riding on you. And you're way behind.

That's the pressure that weighed on Georgia's Stacy Sheppard in the 1994 NCAA tennis championships. With the other singles matches over, all eyes in UGA's Henry Feild Stadium were on her, but she trailed 4-1 in the third and final set of her match. Lose and the Bulldogs fell behind Stanford 4-2, practically an insurmountable score with the national title going to the first team to win five points.

Sheppard was one of UGA's greatest tennis players. A three-time All-America, she is tied for sixth all-time in career victories with 123, but she was in deep trouble that May afternoon. So how did she respond? Quite nicely, thank you, as she gave the Bulldog Nation a moment for the ages. "With no less than a national title on the line and a vocal crowd providing the extra energy, Sheppard lived what most tennis players only dream" about. She stormed back to win five straight games and take the match 7-6, 5-7, 6-4.

"You never give up until the last point is played," Sheppard said. "You just concentrate on the next point. . . . It was a very intense situation, but I think [Georgia coach] Jeff [Wallace] was more nervous than I was."

"Stacy saved us with an incredible comeback," Wallace said. "It was big. Really big," Stanford Coach Frank Brennan agreed.

Sheppard then teamed with Tina Samara to win the final doubles match and claim the women's first national title 5-4. The spark for the championship, though, came from Sheppard's comeback with all that pressure on her shoulders.

You live every day with pressure. As Elijah did so long ago, you lay it on the line with everybody watching. Your family, coworkers, or employees – they depend on you. You know the pressure of a deadline, of a job evaluation, of taking the risk of asking someone to go out with you, of driving in rush-hour traffic.

Help in dealing with daily pressure is readily available, and the only price you pay for it is your willingness to believe. God will give you the grace to persevere if you ask prayerfully.

And while you may need some convincing, the pressures of daily living are really small potatoes because they all will pass. The real pressure comes in deciding where you will spend eternity because that decision is forever. You can handle that pressure easily enough by deciding for Jesus. Eternity is then taken care of; the pressure's off – forever.

Pressure is for tires.

-- Charles Barkley

The greatest pressure you face in life concerns where you will spend eternity, which can be dealt with by deciding for Jesus.

DAY 80

I CAN'T STAND IT!

Read Exodus 32:1-20.

"[Moses'] anger burned and he threw the tablets out of his hands, breaking them to pieces at the foot of the mountain" (v. 19).

Perhaps no athlete in Georgia football history spent more of his time in Athens being frustrated than did D.J. Shockley.

Shockley came to Georgia in 2001 as one of the nation's most highly recruited quarterbacks and Mark Richt's first signee only to find David Greene there, a four-year starter who became the winningest quarterback in Division 1-A history. By 2002, it was clear to everyone – including Shockley – that he was not going to be the starting quarterback at Georgia until Greene left.

He considered transferring, but decided not to even though his own coaches admitted he could start anywhere else. And so he waited, cheering his teammates on, holding a clipboard on the sideline, and admitting that it was frustrating, but always handling himself with class and making the most of his playing opportunities. "He waited patiently, . . . never saying 'I ought to play more' or anything like that," Dan Magill said.

Eventually Greene did graduate and Shockley got his chance. He had one shot, one season, to show the nation what he could do. And did he ever! In 2005, he threw 21 touchdown passes – only Greene and Eric Zeier have thrown more in a season – and finished first in the SEC in passing efficiency. Offensive coordinator Neil Callaway said Shockley's "extremely strong character" "rubbed off on our whole football team." Under Shockley's leadership, the 2005 Dogs won the SEC championship.

That one marvelous season and the way he handled the preceding frustrating ones established D.J. Shockley as one of the most beloved and respected of all Bulldog quarterbacks.

The traffic light catches you when you're running late for work. The bureaucrat gives you red tape when you want assistance. Your daughter refuses to take her homework seriously. Makes your blood boil, doesn't it?

Frustration is part of God's testing ground that is life. Much of our frustration today may result from the people we're attempting to lead as Moses' did, but often the wall we bang our heads against is built by organizations, bureaucracies, and machines.

What's important is not that we encounter frustration -- that's a given -- but how we handle it. Do we respond with curses, screams, and violence? Or with a deep breath, a silent prayer, and calm persistence and patience?

It may be difficult to imagine Jesus stuck in traffic or waiting for hours in a long line. It is not difficult, however, to imagine how he would act in such situations, and, thus, to know exactly how we should respond. No matter how frustrated we are.

A life of frustration is inevitable for any coach whose main enjoyment is winning.

-- NFL Hall of Fame coach Chuck Noll

Frustration is a vexing part of life, but God expects us to handle it gracefully.

DAY 81

ROCK SOLID

Read Luke 6:46-49.

"I will show you what he is like who comes to me and hears my words and puts them into practice. He is like a man building a house, who dug down deep and laid the foundation on rock" (vv. 47-48).

Janet Harris is the foundation.

Since 1981 when the NCAA took over women's basketball, Georgia is one of only four schools to have a winning record every season. The team is fourth in the country in total wins during that time. Heading into the 2009-2010 season, the Lady Dogs have been in all but two NCAA tournaments, the third highest total in the country. They have advanced to 17 Sweet Sixteens, eight Elite Eights, five Final Fours, and two championship games. They have averaged about 24 wins a season, fourth in the country, have been ranked in the top 10 in more than half of the AP polls, and have won a combined 11 SEC championships and SEC Tournament titles, second only to Tennessee.

The Lady Dogs have been great because they have been consistent: one coach in Andy Landers (He came to Athens in 1979.) and a long list of great players that all started with Harris, a four-time All-America from 1982-85. She set eight school records and is still Georgia's career scoring and rebounding leader. In 1993, when Harris joined Teresa Edwards and Katrina McClain in having her jersey number retired, Landers declared that Harris "put our program on the map. She gave us the credibility" the program needed to be great.

Players today come to Athens expecting to be a part of a winner because of the foundation that was laid for greatness – and Janet Harris started it.

Like the University of Georgia's entire athletics program – including women's basketball -- your life is an ongoing project, a work in progress. As with any complex construction job, if your life is to be stable, it must have a solid foundation, which holds everything up and keeps everything together.

R. Alan Culpepper said in *The New Interpreter's Bible*, "We do not choose whether we will face severe storms in life; we only get to choose the foundation on which we will stand." In other words, tough times are inevitable. If your foundation isn't rock-solid, you will have nothing on which to stand as those storms buffet you, nothing to keep your life from flying apart into a cycle of disappointment and destruction.

But when the foundation is solid and sure, you can take the blows, stand strong, recover, and live with joy and hope. Only one foundation is sure and foolproof: Jesus Christ. Everything else you build upon will fail you.

When I was younger, I thought that the key to success was just hard work. But the real foundation is faith.

-- Former NFL player Howard Twilley

In the building of your life, you must start with a good, solid foundation, or the first trouble that shows up will knock you down.

DAY 82

COMEBACK KID

Read Acts 9:1-22.

"All those who heard him were astonished and asked, 'Isn't he the man who raised havoc in Jerusalem among those who call on this name?'" (v. 21)

In the spring of 1980, he lost his scholarship for pushing a coach. In the summer he was told after a car wreck that he would never play football again. That November, he made the most legendary play in the history of Georgia football.

Academic counselor Curt Fludd caught Lindsay Scott and his girlfriend arguing in Scott's dormitory room where she wasn't supposed to be. Scott shoved Fludd, and Vince Dooley took Scott's scholarship away for a year. "The moment I pushed him, I was sorry," Scott said later. "I hated myself for what I had done."

Late that summer, Scott was headed home to Jesup, his mind drifting onto fall practice, which would soon begin, and he lost control of the car. He suffered a concussion and three broken bones in his foot. A doctor told Scott's mom that the injuries had ended his football career.

That he was in the starting lineup for the season opener against Tennessee was a miracle. Lindsay Scott came back all the way on Nov. 8, 1980, in Jacksonville with the play that propelled Georgia to the national championship. 21-20 Florida. Less than two minutes to play. Florida players doing the funky chicken on the sidelines. Third and 93. Buck Belue to Lindsay Scott over the middle – and the race was on. The stadium falls apart; Larry Munson falls out of his chair in the broadcasting booth as he screams "Run, Lindsay!" and "Lindsay Scott! Lindsay Scott! Lindsay Scott!"

In the end zone, Scott shouted, "I'm the luckiest football player in the world today." After the game, he said, "I felt the bottom had fallen out at one time on me, but now I was back."

Lindsay Scott's comeback was complete.

Life will have its setbacks whether they result from personal failures or from forces and people beyond your control. Being a Christian and a faithful follower of Jesus Christ doesn't insulate you from getting into deep trouble. Maybe financial problems suffocated you. A serious illness put you on the sidelines. Or your family was hit with a great tragedy.

Life is a series of victories and defeats. Winning isn't about avoiding defeat; it's about getting back up to compete again. It's about making a comeback of your own.

When you avail yourself of God's grace and God's power, your comeback is always greater than your setback. You are never too far behind, and it's never too late in life's game for Jesus to lead you to victory, to turn trouble into triumph.

As it was with Lindsay Scott and with Paul, it's not how you start that counts; it's how you finish.

Turn a setback into a comeback.

-- Former football coach Billy Brewer

In life, victory is truly a matter of how you finish and whether you finish with Jesus at your side.

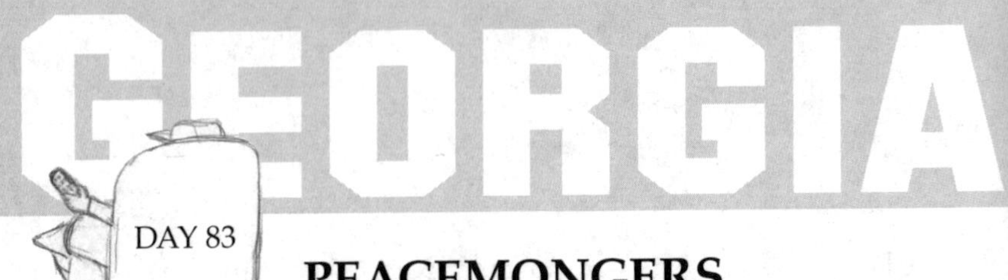

PEACEMONGERS

Read Hebrews 12:14-17.

"Make every effort to live in peace with all men and to be holy" (v. 14).

A Georgia football player once slugged it out with an opposing coach -- during a game.

Harold Ketron was a rugged lineman who lettered in 1901, '02, '03, and '06. He was a team captain and was so good that when he was the only returning player in 1906, *The Atlanta Constitution* said Georgia would be all right because "Ketron is a whole team in himself."

For "War Eagle" Ketron, "a good fist-fight was an integral part of a hotly-contested game." He didn't always come out on top. "I saw him take some good lickings," his brother, Grover, said, "but I never saw him shy away from anyone."

In the 1903 game against powerhouse Vanderbilt, Vandy Coach J.R. Henry spent a great deal of his time running onto the field to urge the refs to watch Ketron closely. As his teammates told it, Ketron "would grab his man by the hair and spit tobacco juice in his face." The enraged opponent would frequently retaliate by swinging at Ketron, but since the refs couldn't see the stream of tobacco that started the whole fray, Ketron's victim would draw a penalty.

Finally Henry ran onto the field one time too many, and a fight broke out. A reporter rushed onto the field and "found Ketron and Coach Henry slugging away at each other." Later, "Ketron was struggling with two policemen, one of whom was throttling him and the other attempting to hold him, while Coach Henry was being forcibly taken off the field" by the law. Since the game was played in Atlanta and not Nashville, Ketron stayed in the game while Coach Henry was arrested and hauled downtown.

Perhaps you've never been quite as prone to brawling and fighting as was "War Eagle" Ketron. But maybe you retaliated when you got one elbow too many in a pickup basketball game. Or maybe you and your spouse or your teenager get into it occasionally, shouting and saying cruel things. Or road rage may be a part of your life.

While we do seem to live in a more belligerent and more confrontational society than ever before, fighting is still not the solution to a problem. Rather, it only escalates the whole confrontation, leaving wounded pride, intransigence, and simmering hatred in its wake. Actively seeking and making peace is the way to a solution that lasts and heals broken relationships and aching hearts.

Peacemaking is not as easy as fighting, but it is much more courageous and a lot less painful. It is also the Jesus thing to do.

No matter what the other fellow does on the field, don't let him lure you into a fight. Uphold your dignity.

-- Legendary Alabama football coach Frank Thomas

Making peace instead of fighting takes courage and strength; it's also what Jesus would do.

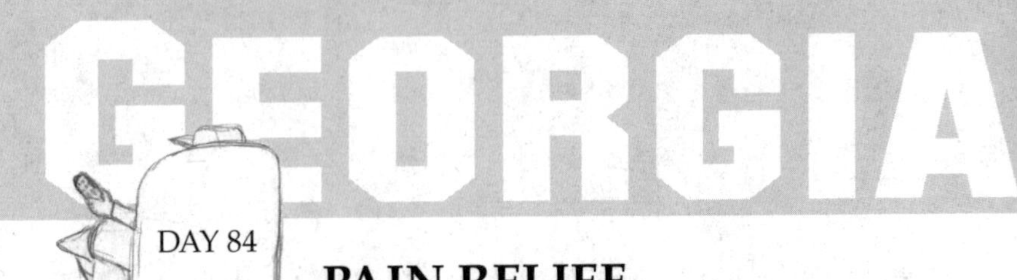

PAIN RELIEF

Read 2 Corinthians 1:3-7.

"Just as the sufferings of Christ flow over into our lives, so also through Christ our comfort overflows" (v. 5).

No way you can pull off a gymnastics routine with a broken toe, right? Unless you're a Georgia Bulldog and your team needs your help to win the SEC Championship.

At the 1991 conference championships, Georgia and Alabama were neck-in-neck. Alabama had completed its four events, and the GymDogs had the floor to finish. Georgia had only five gymnasts available for the event since Lisa Alicea was nursing a broken toe. She didn't even warm up.

When a Georgia gymnast fell, the Alabama gymnasts began their victory celebration. With no sixth gymnast, Georgia had to count the low score that came with the fall. Alabama had the title in the bag.

Hold on. Coach Suzanne Yoculan said she was never sure why she did it, but she had listed Alicea in the lineup. Thus, she was available to compete.

After the fall, Yoculan "huddled with Lisa and watered-down her routine to one that would provide the needed 9.45 for Georgia to win the championship, but would minimize stress on the broken toe." Still, the toe was broken, Alicea hadn't practiced a full routine in weeks, and she would have to hit the routine to secure the points the GymDogs needed to win. It was a long shot at best.

Hey, these are the Dawgs we're talking about here. Her teammates fidgeted, the coaches winced, and Alicea performed with gritted teeth the whole way, but she nailed a 9.45. The GymDogs were the SEC champions.

"This is the happiest moment of my life," Alicea declared after the meeting. She had certainly experienced some of the most painful moments of her life.

Since you live on earth and not in heaven, you are forced – as Lisa Alicea was -- to play with pain. Whether it's a car wreck that left you shattered, the end of a relationship that left you battered, or a loved one's death that left you tattered -- pain finds you and challenges you to keep going.

While God's word teaches that you will reap what you sow, life also teaches that pain and hardship are not necessarily the result of personal failure. Pain in fact can be one of the tools God uses to mold your character and change your life.

What are you to do when you are hit full-speed by the awful pain that seems to choke the very will to live out of you? Where is your consolation, your comfort, and your help?

In almighty God, whose love will never fail. When life knocks you to your knees, you're closer to God than ever before.

It hurts up to a point and then it doesn't get any worse.

-- Ultramarathon runner Ann Trason

When life hits you with pain, you can always turn to God for comfort, consolation, and hope.

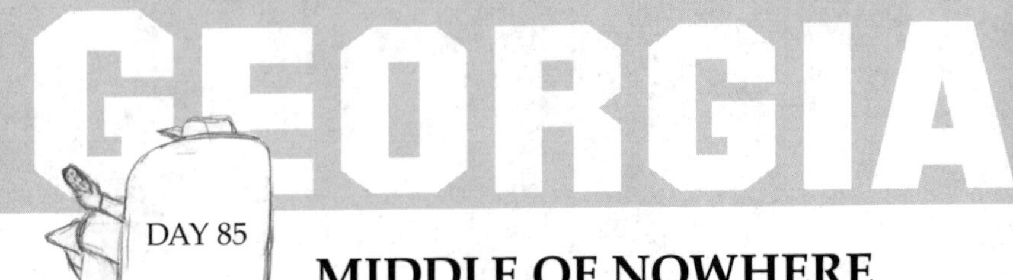

MIDDLE OF NOWHERE

Read Genesis 28:10-22.

"When Jacob awoke from his sleep, he thought, 'Surely the Lord is in this place, and I was not aware of it'" (v. 16).

Right smack dab in the middle of nowhere, Georgia found one of its greatest athletes ever. Or rather, a traveling salesman did.

In the spring of 1928, an ice-cream salesman trying to find Carnesville came to an unmarked fork in the road and sat there for a moment, perplexed. He spotted a "husky, freckle-faced, auburn-haired" boy beside the road plowing a cotton field and asked for directions.

To the salesman's amazement, "the boy picked up the plow with his right arm and pointed the way to Carnesville." A staunch Georgia fan, the greatly impressed ice-cream man struck up a conversation with the boy and learned that the youngster had been a three-sport star in high school. He had played football and baseball and had thrown the javelin in track.

To his discomfiture, the salesman also learned the boy had been offered a football scholarship to Clemson. Then the youngster offered one additional piece of information: He preferred to attend Georgia.

The salesman reported his find to Georgia head football coach Harry Mehre; he contacted the plowboy, who subsequently passed on Clemson and came to Athens. The boy's name was Spurgeon Chandler.

Chandler starred as the left halfback from 1929-31. He was also the team's punter and an excellent defensive back. He was a star baseball player, too, signing with the New York Yankees after his last baseball season with Georgia in 1932. He spent much of his signing bonus riding a cab to his classes on Ag Hill. Chandler won 109 games in the majors before arm problems forced his retirement. He was 20-4 in 1943 and was the American League MVP – this youngster discovered in the middle of nowhere.

Ever been to Meigs? Bushnell? Or Shoulderbone, just down the road from Veazey and Mosquito Crossing?

They are among the many small communities, some of them nothing more than crossroads, that dot the Georgia countryside. Not on any interstate highway or even a four-lane highway, they seem to be in the middle of nowhere, the type of place where Spurgeon Chandler could be found plowing a field. They're just hamlets we zip through on our way to somewhere important.

But don't be misled; those villages are indeed special and wonderful. That's because God is in Aska and Roopville just as he is in Athens, downtown Atlanta, Columbus, and Savannah. Even when you are far off the roads well traveled, you are with God.

As Jacob discovered one rather astounding morning, the middle of nowhere is, in fact, holy ground -- because God is there.

The middle of nowhere is the place that teaches you that crossing the goal line first is not as important as the course you took to get there.
– Dive instructor Ridlon Kiphart

No matter how far off the beaten path you travel, you are still on holy ground because God is there.

DAY 86

CLOTHES HORSE

Read Genesis 37:1-11.

"Israel loved Joseph more than all his children, because he was the son of his old age: and he made him a coat of many colours" (v. 3) (KJV).

One thing about the Georgia football team you can be sure of: They'll be dressed to kill when they take the field.

Among the most striking features of the Georgia uniform through the years have been the silver britches and the unique "G" helmet. Wally Butts, who took over as head coach in 1939, came up with the silver pants, which, when paired with bright red jerseys, made for an eye-catching uniform.

When Vince Dooley arrived in 1964, he ditched the silver britches in favor of white pants as part of a uniform makeover. He resurrected the silver britches in 1980, though, and the Dogs won the national championship. Just a coincidence, surely.

The now-famous "G" helmet was also part of Dooley's 1964 uniform redesign. He discussed with his staff that a "forward-looking 'G'" would be appropriate for the team. The wife of new backfield coach and former player John Donaldson (1945-48) designed the logo in accordance with Dooley's specifications that included a black "G" on a white background and a red helmet. Noticing a similarity to the "G" of the Green Bay Packers despite the difference in colors, Dooley secured permission for the new emblem, which made its initial appearance in the first game of

1964 and has remained Georgia's most visible logo ever since.

Speaking of clothes, Uga's jerseys are custom-made each season from the same material used for the players' jerseys. His old ones are destroyed.

The uniforms may change, but the winning goes on.

Contemporary society proclaims that it's all about the clothes. Buy that new suit or dress, those new shoes, and all the sparkling accessories, and you'll be a new person. The changes are only cosmetic, though; under those clothes, you're the same person. Changing the style or colors of its uniforms won't make a football team any better. And consider Joseph, prancing about in his pretty new clothes; he was still a spoiled tattletale whose brothers despised him.

Jesus never taught that we should run around half-naked or wear only second-hand clothes from the local mission. He did warn us, though, against making consumer items such as clothes a priority in our lives.

A follower of Christ seeks to emulate Jesus not through material, superficial means such as wearing special clothing like a robe and sandals. Rather, the disciple desires to match Jesus' inner beauty and serenity -- whether the clothes the Christian wears are the sables of a king or the rags of a pauper.

You can't call [golf] a sport. You don't run, jump, you don't shoot, you don't pass. All you have to do is buy some clothes that don't match.
-- Former major leaguer Steve Sax

Where Jesus is concerned,
clothes don't make the person; faith does.

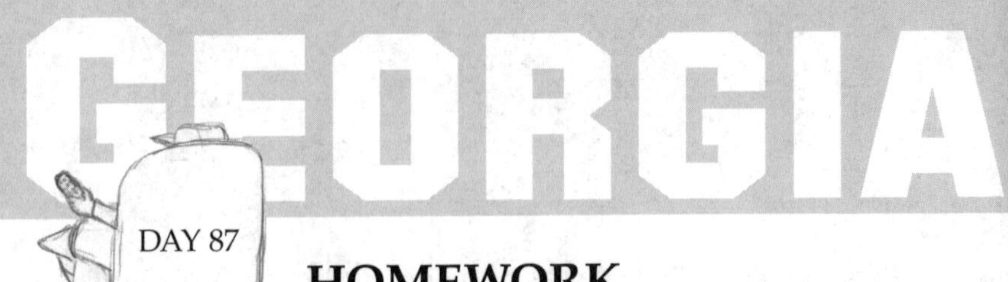

HOMEWORK

Read Joshua 1:1-9.

"Do not let this Book of the Law depart from your mouth; meditate on it day and night, so that you may be careful to do everything written in it. Then you will be prosperous and successful" (v. 8).

Alec Kessler always did his homework.

Kessler, who died unexpectedly in 2007, was the senior captain of Georgia's 1990 SEC champions and was a first-round NBA pick. He led the champions in both rebounding and scoring, and UPI named him second-team All-America.

Despite his basketball success, Kessler's "academic performance fairly dwarfed his athletic exploits." Kessler dreamed of becoming an orthopedic surgeon, so at Georgia he majored in microbiology upon the advice of his older brother, Chad, who suggested the grueling coursework would serve a medical student well. Kessler threw himself into the biology labwork as wholeheartedly as he threw his body around the basketball court.

His academic success drew national recognition his sophomore season when he was named a first team Academic All-America, and he became "a symbol, not only for Georgia basketball, but also for everything that is good about college athletics." Both his junior and senior years, he was named the Academic All-American of the Year, an honor that includes athletes in all sports. "Never before," wrote Tim Hix, "had Georgia had such an accomplished player" in both basketball and the classroom.

And the secret of Kessler's success? Hard work. Brother Chad said, "I can honestly say that Alec is one of the most focused and dedicated and driven people I've ever known. . . . He could sit down and study for six straight hours."

Alec Kessler did his homework.

One of the most enduring illusions of adolescence is that once you graduate, the homework ends. Life requires constant, ongoing study, however. In many ways, you assemble a life much as you do a bicycle for your children. You know the drill; even with parts scattered all over the garage, you work undismayed because you can read the instructions and follow them. With the bicycle assembled and ready to race the wind, you nod in satisfaction. Mission completed.

Wouldn't it be great if life, too, had an instruction book, a set of directions that can lead you to a productive, rewarding life so that as its end you can nod in satisfaction and declare "Mission completed"?

It does. Life's instruction book is probably by your bed or on a living room table. It's the Bible, given to you by God to guide you through life. But for it to do you any good, you must read it; you must do your homework.

Sooner or later, I knew a bunch of school teachers would decide athletes had to study and become educated like the other students.

-- Lewis Grizzard

The Bible is God's instruction book with directions on how to assemble your life.

A HOLLYWOOD ENDING

Read Luke 24:1-12.

"Why do you look for the living among the dead? He is not here; he has risen!" (vv. 5, 6a)

Try selling this to Hollywood: Football star gets injured badly. Recruiters back off. In last second, he wins game against favored team with longest kick in school history. Too hokey even for Hollywood, right? But it's true.

Playing quarterback and doubling as the kicker at Redan High, Kevin Butler hurt his knee on the last play of the first game of his senior year. Many of the recruiters disappeared, but Georgia stayed with him.

He secured his place in Bulldog lore on a hot September day in 1984 against second-ranked Clemson. With 11 seconds left, the score was tied at 23, and Georgia faced fourth down at the Clemson 43. Hail Mary time. But coach Vince Dooley simply looked at Butler and said, "Field goal."

Huh? 60+ yards? Even Butler admitted the decision "freaked out the people in the stands." Perhaps nobody was more freaked out than announcer Larry Munson: "So we'll try to kick one 100,000 miles. We're holding it on our own 49 and a half! Gonna try to kick it 60 yards plus a foot and a half!" And that's exactly what Butler did. Munson again: "And Butler kicked a long one! . . . Eleven seconds! I can't believe what he did!"

"I knew it was going to be good" the moment he hit it, Butler said. So he ran down to the student section and dropped to his knees to lead one of the most frenzied celebrations in Bulldog history.

Georgia won 26-23, the game Bulldog fans voted in 2004 as the greatest game ever played in Sanford Stadium -- Hollywood ending and all.

The world tells us that happy endings are for fairy tales and the movies, that reality is Cinderella dying in childbirth and her prince getting killed in a peasant uprising. But that's just another of the world's lies.

The truth is that Jesus Christ has been producing happy endings for almost two millennia. That's because in Jesus lies the power to change and to rescue a life no matter how desperate the situation. Jesus is the master at putting shattered lives back together, of healing broken hearts and broken relationships, of resurrecting lost dreams.

And as for living happily ever after – God really means it. The greatest Hollywood ending of them all was written on a Sunday morning centuries ago when Jesus left a tomb and death behind. With faith in Jesus, your life can have that same ending. You live with God in peace, joy, and love – forever. The End.

This field, this game, is a part of our past, Ray. It reminds us of all that once was good, and that could be again.

-- *James Earl Jones in* Field of Dreams

Hollywood's happy endings are products of imagination; the happy endings Jesus produces are real and are yours for the asking.

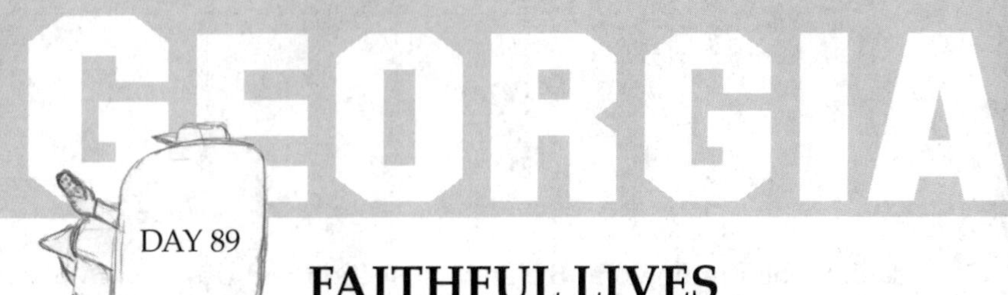

FAITHFUL LIVES

Read Hebrews 11:1-12.

"Faith is the substance of things hoped for, the evidence of things not seen" (v. 1 NKJV).

In 1986, a death changed Mark Richt's life.

He was a graduate assistant at Florida State when a Seminole offensive tackle was shot and killed in Tallahassee. Understandably, the team and the players were deeply shaken, perhaps Richt most of all. He turned to head coach Bobby Bowden for comfort, and Bowden turned his young assistant toward the ultimate source of all comfort. In the process Richt found a new life.

Richt became a devout Christian, studying the Bible, attending church more often, and trying to live his life the way God wants him to. Today, Richt doesn't separate his job as head coach of the Georgia Bulldogs from his devotion to God. "My motivation daily is to try and honor Him by working as hard as I possibly can and succeeding in whatever I do," he said.

While Richt doesn't leave his faith at his office door, neither does he attempt to push his faith on others in deference to the complexities of his position at a public university. "If [players] come to me, or want to accept Jesus Christ, then I will share with them. But in no way am I trying to force [my faith] on anyone," he said.

One of the most striking illustrations of how Richt's faith plays out in his job is his calm in the midst of bedlam, a desirable trait that many coaches lack. "He maintains a steady emotional keel in practice, during games, and away from football, which allows him to make clear decisions and focus on the task at hand," wrote Brian Curtis.

All-American David Pollack – also a committed Christian -- once observed how encouraging it was that his coach was "open about faith. That a man of God is running the program." And so it is encouraging for Dog fans and Jesus fans wherever they are.

Your faith forms the heart and soul of what you are. Faith in people, things, ideologies, and concepts to a large extent determines how you spend your life. You believe in the Georgia Bulldogs, in your family, in the basic goodness of Americans, in freedom and liberty, and in abiding by the law. These beliefs mold you and make you the person you are.

This is all great stuff, of course, that makes for decent human beings and productive lives. None of it, however, is as important as what you believe about Jesus. To have faith in Jesus is to believe his message of hope and salvation as recorded in the Bible.

True faith in Jesus, however, has an additional component; it must also include a personal commitment to him. In other words, you don't just believe in Jesus; you live for him.

Faith in Jesus does more than shape your life; it determines your eternity.

I never search for a reason why; I have faith in the Lord's purpose.
– Former major leaguer Willie Stargell

You believe in Jesus, but you also do much more:
You live for him.

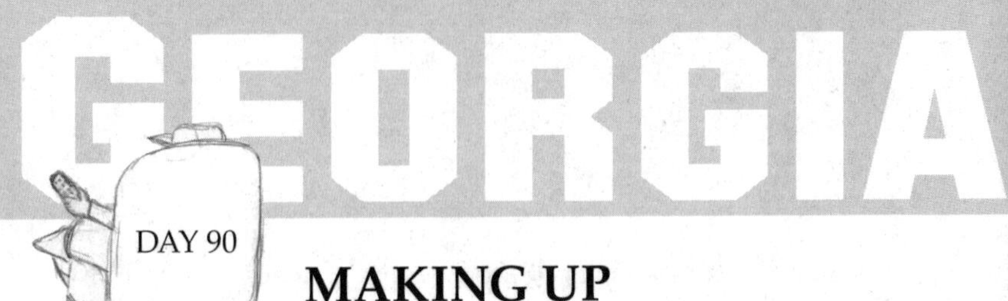

MAKING UP

Read Matthew 5:21-24.

"If you are offering your gift at the altar and there remember that your brother has something against you, leave your gift there in front of the altar. First go and be reconciled to your brother" (vv. 23-24).

The Georgia-Georgia Tech baseball rivalry once got so heated the student bodies signed a peace treaty promising not to shoot opposing team members during a game or drop laxatives into their water buckets.

In May 1919, in a game at Grant Field, Georgia led 2-1 in the bottom of the ninth, but Tech had a runner at third with one out. That's when Tech's band left the stands, gathered near the field, and cranked up full blast in an attempt to rattle Georgia pitcher David Satterfield. It didn't work; Satterfield struck out the final two batters. The Tech "stunt" and the Georgia win led to "general misbehavior by both sides" all afternoon and into the night.

Tommy Philpot then embarrassed Tech with an 8-0 no-hitter the next day, and "boisterous behavior was the order of the day" again. Calm heads realized something had to be done. Both schools sent student representatives to the other's campus for conferences to draw up what was in effect a peace treaty. *The Atlanta Journal* headlined its report "Tech and Georgia Students Smoke Pipe of Peace" and said from now on the "old enemies" would limit their battling to the athletic field.

Among other matters, the student bodies agreed not to shoot opposing team members during a game and not to poison them with laxatives in their water buckets. The freshmen agreed not to steal caps from each other and then display those caps during baseball games. They also agreed unanimously "that the former German Kaiser should be hung."

College sports just wouldn't be as much fun if we didn't have rivalries with teams we love to insult, rail against, and whip the daylights out of. Our personal relationships are totally different, however, though sometimes a spirited disagreement with someone we love is worth it because the kissing and making up is so much fun.

Making up carries an inherent problem because for reconciliation to occur, somebody must make the first move, which is always the hardest one. So often relationships in our lives are fractured simply because no one has the courage to be the first to attempt to make things right. We hide behind our wounded pride or injured feelings and allow a priceless relationship to wither and die.

The model in such a situation is Jesus. He not only told us to offer a hand and a hug, he lived it, surrendering his life so we could all get right with God.

Sport provides communities the opportunity to come together and reconcile; sport teaches important values such as respect, tolerance, solidarity, teamwork and fairness.

– Liberian official Adolf Ogi

Reconciliation takes courage; just ask Jesus, who died to get you right with God.

GEORGIA

NOTES
(by devotion number)

1 After classes each day . . . romping aimlessly around.: John F. Stegeman, *The Ghosts of Herty Field* (Athens: The University of Georgia Press, 1997), p. 2.

1 In Baltimore, he had . . . specimens for the first team.": Stegeman, p. 3.

2 He started the first nine games . . . Bobo was benched.: Chip Towers, "Redemption," http://www.onlineathens.com/1996/111796/1117.dogs.html.

2 With third and 18 at the Auburn 31 . . . the first of his career.": Chip Towers, "Bobo, Edwards Sparkle in Four-Overtime Victory," *The Augusta Chronicle*, Nov. 17, 1996, http://chronicle.augusta.com/stories/111796/georgia.html, March 29, 2009.

2 Completing 21 of 37 passes . . . "the rejuvenated Bobo.": Marc Lancaster, "Bobo, Edwards Rally Dogs," http://www.onlineathens.com/1996/111796/1117.rally.html.

2 "It's the best feeling . . . the biggest win of my life.": Towers, "Redemption."

3 the greatest dunker he ever saw . . . UGA's own Herb White.: Tim Hix, *Hoop Tales: Georgia Bulldogs Men's Basketball* (Guilford, CN: The Globe Pequot Press, 2006), p. 164.

3 White's fame, though, came from . . . and English conceded.: Hix, *Hoop Tales*, p. 164.

4 Terry Hoage was the star . . . I was that bad.": Tony Barnhart, *What It Means to Be a Bulldog* (Chicago: Triumph Books, 2004), p. 264.

4 After the Clemson game . . . the second half started: Barnhart, *What It Means*, p. 265.

4 "I just remember my teammates . . . a time when they didn't do that.": Barnhart, *What It Means*, p. 267.

5 for $1 a year.: Jesse Outlar, *Between the Hedges* (Huntsville, AL: The Strode Publishers, 1974), p. 29.

5 He didn't want the job . . . choice of school officials: Outlar, p. 35.

5 In the Tech game that season, . . . the details of obtaining them.": Outlar, p. 28.

5 When Whitney's assistant coach . . . to a 6-0 upset.: Outlar, p. 29.

5 His most famous bit . . . untouched for a touchdown.: Loran Smith with Lewis Grizzard, *Glory! Glory*! (Atlanta: Peachtree Publishers Limited, 1981), p. 6.

6 The band started in 1905 . . . called the Bulldog Banners.: "The History of the University of Georgia Redcoat Band 1905-2005," http://bands.music.uga.edu/redcoata/history.php, March 29, 2009.

7 "had no opportunity. . . . from 1961 to 1963.": Vince Dooley with Loran Smith, *Dooley's Dawgs* (Atlanta: Longstreet Press, 2003), p. 41.

7 "I know it was tough for him, . . . what he went through,": Dooley with Smith, p. 42.

7 "If he had gotten mad . . . to watch a recruit, Edgar Chandler,: Dooley with Smith, p. 42.

7 Johnny Griffith shwoed a lot of class in that situation.: Dooley with Smith, p. 42.

8 his success as a distance runner . . . Amateur Athletic Union mile race.: Dan Magill, *Dan Magill's Bull-Doggerel* (Atlanta: Longstreet Press, Inc., 1993), p. 16.

8 with Tate and Young matching each other . . . "a smarter coach than I did.":

Magill, p. 17.

9 Both Georgia's number-one quarterback, . . . quarterback Paul Gilbert, a senior from Athens.: Magill, p. 93.

9 Gilbert had begun the 1988 season . . . and passed for 245 yards.: Magill, p. 94.

10 "an absolutely brutal first half . . . handed to us": Barnhart, *What It Means*, p. 334.

10 "Greene took the snap . . . the smaller Auburn defender": Tim Hix, *Stadium Stories: Georgia Bulldogs* (Guilford, CN: The Globe Pequot Press, 2006), p. 74.

10 "It was just pitch and catch,": Hix, *Stadium Stories*, p. 76.

11 Macy determined to get stronger . . . and vigorously working out.: Suzanne Yoculan and Bill Donaldson, *Perfect 10* (Athens: Hill Street Press, 2006), p. 76.

11 "Not one time did it cross . . . do a handstand on bars: Yoculan and Donaldson, p. 78.

11 She was down to about 80 pounds . . . watch everyone else work out.: Yoculan and Donaldson, p. 79.

11 Even after Macy gained . . . "the wake-up call.": Yoculan and Donaldson, p. 80.

11 her dad said Yoculan's tough-love approach saved his daughter's life.: Yoculan and Donaldson, p. 82.

12 "a joke, a total joke.": J.C. Clemons, "No. 24 Georgia Women Miss NCAA Field of 48," *The Atlanta Journal/The Atlanta Constitution*, March 16, 1992, p. E1.

12 "What criteria? The criteria . . . " a 19-9 record and an unranked team.: Marion Manuel and Scott M. Reid, "Georgia Rejects NWIT; Tech Jumps at Invitation," *The Atlanta Journal/The Atlanta Constitution*, March 16, 1992, p. E4.

12 five Pac-10 teams were selected, though only one was ranked in the top 25.: Ailene Voisin, "NCAA Bubble Bursts for Tournament Heroines Tech, Georgia," *The Atlanta Journal/The Atlanta Constitution*, March 16, 1992, p. E5.

12 "No Lady Bulldogs. . . . No justice.": Voisin, "NCAA Bubble Bursts."

12 None of us wants justice . . . we'd all go to hell.: Bettinger, Jim & Julie S. *The Book of Bowden* (Nashville: TowleHouse Publishing, 2001), p. 69.

13 As faculty chairman of athletics, . . . insisted be named Sanford Field.: Hix, *Stadium Stories*, p. 106.

13 By the 1920s, though, . . . and looked down into a gully.: Hix, *Stadium Stories*, p. 107.

13 The area was so steeply sloped . . . a firing range for the rifle team.: Hix, *Stadium Stories*, p. 108.

13 "a wild bottomland," . . . "a damp and shadowy valley.": Wilton Sharpe, *Bulldog Madness* (Nashville: Cumberland House, p. 207.

13 As he stood there, Sanford told . . . It's a natural.": Hix, *Stadium Stories*, p. 107.

13 When Sanford first presented . . . athletics board voted against him.: Hix, *Stadium Stories*, p. 108.

13 Professor Sanford wasn't interested so much . . . a football field in the hollow.: Sharpe, p. 207.

14 "probably the most influential men in the history of college tennis,": Norman Arey, "Georgia Names Tennis Complex for Dan Magill," *The Atlanta Journal/The Atlanta Constitution*, May 14, 1993, p. E3.

14 "had the brainstorm to put on . . . by a creek in Oconee County,": Magill, p. 157.

14 a good friend had snared a five-foot timber rattler.: Magill, p. 158.

14 In the local paper . . . quit asking for a refund.": Magill, p. 159.
14 But the snakes never did fight.: Magill, p. 160.
15 Hester was a three-time . . . as an assistant golf coach: "Georgia Biographies: Kelley Hester," georgiadogs.com: Women's Golf: Coaches. http://www.georgia-dogs.com/ViewArticle.dmbl?SPSID=40683&SPSID=3578&DB_OEM, Aug. 14, 2007.
15 "It's just where I always . . . a coach and ultimately coach here.": Michael A. Lough, "Two Paths, One Hometown," *The Telegraph*, Aug. 6, 2007, p. 3C.
16 "desperation play,": Outlar, p. 127.
16 "C'mon, [Coach Dooley] didn't call that . . . . We're going to run it. Flea flicker !": Barnhart, *What It Means*, p. 124.
16 When the play was installed . . . "run it in a game!": Barnhart, *What It Means*, p. 148.
16 When you run trick plays . . . folks question your sanity.: Bettinger, p. 32.
17 The football players didn't have . . . with a bow and arrow;: Vince Dooley with Blake Giles, "1980: The Pig," *Echoes of Georgia Football*, ed. Ken Samelson (Chicago: Triumph Books, 2006), p. 162.
17 Hudson had some experience with barbecuing hogs.: Dooley with Giles, p. 163.
17 some freshman players dumped . . . license plate number: Dooley with Giles, p. 165.
17 Coach Vince Dooley revoked . . . during the heat of the day.: Dooley with Giles, p. 166.
17 The incident became a catalyst . . . a lot of people together.": Dooley with Giles, p. 168.
17 Ros said everybody on the team . . . to pay for the pig.": Smith with Grizzard, p. 81.
17 Coach Erk Russell told him he was glad the whole thing happened.: Dooley with Giles, p. 168.
17 We had some good people, . . . we built on the hog story.: Dooley with Giles, p. 168.
18 "If somebody's stupid enough . . . I'll do it,": Dave Kindred, "Germ Study a Model Role for Volleyball 'Gym Rat,'" *The Atlanta Journal/The Atlanta Constitution*, Jan. 21, 1996, p. E3.
18 In 1995, *Glamour* magazine . . . "All I do is play volleyball.": Kindred.
18 "I love pathogens," . . . "to want to make a difference.": Kindred.
19 "the biggest touchdown pass I ever threw.": Outlar, p. 107.
19 "We were really nervous . . . I couldn't believe it.": Outlar, p. 107.
19 "Somehow during all that excitement . . . point did not matter.": Outlar, p. 107.
20 1,355 of them. . . . surrounding the fenced field": Mark Schlabach, "Lady Dogs Top Panthers 4-0 in Debut," *The Atlanta Journal/The Atlanta Constitution*, Sept. 4, 1995, p. D2.
20 "We don't know what to expect. . . . to be part of something new.": Wendy Parker, "Soccer Gets Kick-Start at Georgia," *The Atlanta Journal/The Atlanta Constitution*, Sept. 1, 1995, p. E1.
20 "It's the best thing . . . many people watching before.": Schlabach.
21 Players letting their hair . . . they didn't wear helmets: Clyde Bolton, *War Eagle* (Huntsville, AL: The Strode Publishers, 1973), p. 45.
21 Spectators rushing onto the field and getting in the players' way.: Bolton, *War*

Eagle, p. 49.

21 A watermelon-shaped ball, too big to hold in your hand and pass.: Clyde Bolton, *The Crimson Tide* (Huntsville, AL: The Strode Publishers, 1972), p. 46.

21 Games called on account of darkness: Bolton, *War Eagle*, p. 48.

21 A nose guard was about . . . if he provided them himself.: Bolton, *The Crimson Tide*, p. 46.

21 Scrambling to find somebody . . . rather than a level one: Bolton, *War Eagle*, p. 50.

21 A player hiding the ball under a jersey. No scoreboard: Bolton, *War Eagle*, p. 69.

21 A player kicking . . . on his helmet: Bolton, *War Eagle*, p. 78.

21 The length of the halves . . . depending upon the weather: Bolton, *War Eagle*, p. 80.

21 Teammates dragging a tackled ball carrier forward: Bolton, *War Eagle*, p. 81.

21 A Georgia player dressed . . . catching a pass: Bolton, *The Crimson Tide*, p. 37.

21 handles were sewn . . . easier to toss: Bolton, *War Eagle*, p. 81.

22 Thank goodness for Elaine Bailey.": Hix, *Stadium Stories*, p. 72.

22 "most acclaimed, illustrious . . . Georgia football history.": Hix, *Stadium Stories*, p. 72.

22 "the most versatile player at Georgia since the inception of two-platoon football." "All Americans," georgiadogs.com: Football: History: Honors and Awards, http://admin.xosn.attachments1/1581.pdf?SPSID=-46724&SPSID, p. 181.

22 Seven times during the 1998 season . . . a "dinosaur": Hix, *Stadium Stories*, p. 72.

22 "He can do whatever . . . on the football field,": Hix, *Stadium Stories*, p. 72.

22 "She's the center of everything," . . . It never stops with my mom.": Hix, *Stadium Stories*, p. 73.

23 Kim Thompson was so nervous . . . about her uniform: Lya Wodraska, "No Skirting the Issue at UGA," *The Atlanta Journal/The Atlanta Constitution*, Jan. 20, 1993, p. F7.

23 "I was so scared," . . . scoring 32 points.: Wodraska.

23 Thompson's basketball career had her . . . dribble right past them.": Wodraska.

24 He rode to Athens from Macon. . . "we better go back home.": Barnhart, *What It Means*, pp. 7-8.

24 Each year head coach Wally Butts picked . . . he would let you know it.": Barnhart, *What It Means*, p. 8.

24 "My daddy died . . . I was on my own.": Barnhart, *What It Means*, p. 7.

25 "We would have been run off . . . No two uniforms looked alike.": Stegeman, p. 54.

25 "On account of the poor . . . in need of wind.": Stegeman, p. 53.

25 "an old dressing room in the basement of Old College.": Stegeman, p. 54

25 Professor Charles Herty, the "Father . . . "old red dirt field.": Stegeman, p. 38.

25 "a playing field of sorts, bare and stubbly.": Stegeman, p. 1.

25 Herty said the teams won . . . "in the South.": Stegeman, p. 38.

26 "I felt isolated," . . . their open and deep faith.: Jack Wilkinson, "On the Track, Lady Dogs Find Common Ground," *The Atlanta Journal/The Atlanta Constitution*, June 2, 1995, p. E6.

27 Rufus "Cow" Nalley invented the huddle in 1895.: Outlar, p. 21.

27 George "Kid" Woodruff . . . a dollar a year. Outlar, p. 35.

27 he won the SEC championship without any scholarshipped swimmers.: Magill, p. 130.
27 he labeled fullback Ronnie Jenkins . . . over would-be tacklers.: Magill, p. 171.
27 one punched out the opposing . . . officials wouldn't stop him.: Magill, pp. 5-6.
27 There are sports names, . . . I've heard few better.: Sharpe, p. 53.
28 "I really didn't like that idea . . Nobody ever touched him.: Barnhart, *What It Means*, p. 172.
29 In the 1920s, Georgia's . . . "Put him to work," Butts said: Magill, p. 176.
30 she "couldn't run down . . . spit her out every day.": Steve Hummer, "Lycett's Long, Strange Trip Nears an End," *The Atlanta Journal/The Atlanta Constitution*, March 29, 2003, p. E8.
30 "played more like Miss Manner.": Hummer.
30 "None of them was much . . . get better or get killed every day,": Hummer.
30 Lycett made the greatest . . . most dependable three-point shooter: Hummer.
31 Richt confessed he ordered . . . "I wanted the guys to be in a frenzy.": Josh Kendall, "Moreno, Teammates Mount Day-Long Georgia Celebration," *The Telegraph*, Oct. 28, 2007, p. 1C.
31 "We had been playing dull . . . to get everybody going.": Josh Kendall, "Defensive Coaches Braced for Penalty," *The Telegraph*, Oct. 28, 2007, p. 4C.
31 "We were saying, 'Whoa, . . . That's got to be the wrong spot.'": Kendall, "Defensive Coaches Braced for Penalty."
32 All those guys from Georgia are always tough.": Barnhart, *What It Means*, p. 95.
32 "I was so scared that . . . still means something to me.": Barnhart, *What It Means*, p. 95.
33 "Big Jim" received his nickname the day he was born.: McGill, p. 57.
33 He was such a spectacular athlete . . . many an unsuspecting person.": Magill, p. 55.
33 Whatley was an avid fisherman . . . but merely stuns it: Magill, p. 59.
34 After losing to Clemson . . . by which they had beaten Georgia: Bill Cromartie, *Clean Old-Fashioned Hate* (Huntsville, AL: The Strode Publishers, 1977), p. 34.
34 "Eating applies is said to be . . . a large city are unknown.": Stegeman, p. 65.
34 "forty-four bushels of select . . . in their humiliation one bit.: Cromartie, p. 34.
34 Georgia led TCU 40-7 . . . with juice streaming down his face.": Outlar, p. 67.
35 Collins came to Georgia as the next Herschel: Troy Johnson, "Senior Class Creates Lasting Memories," http://www.onlineathens.com/1996/120196/1201.senior.html, Aug. 19, 2003.
35 Collins had perhaps been most famous . . . to fetch his laundry from the dryer: Johnson.
35 his unborn daughter died . . . "a smile on my face": Johnson.
36 He had broken his racket . . . "Totally forgot about me. That hurt.": Scott M. Reid, "Georgia's McGuire Leaving Ailments and Anger Behind," *The Atlanta Journal/The Atlanta Constitution*, May 13, 1993, p. G1.
36 In 1991, he rolled a golf cart, . . . all going to end?": Reid, "Georgia's McGuire."
36 "This year hasn't gone the way . . what I came back for.": Reid, "Georgia's McGuire."
37 Ros was born in Barcelona,. . . "I figured that out".: Smith with Grizzard, p. 83.
37 though at his first lunch break, . . . escorted him to the school lunchroom.: Smith with Grizzard, pp. 83-84.

37 Young Frank Ros needed several . . . only in his middle grades.: Smith with Grizzard, p. 84.
38 Each year Yale scheduled an . . . ran out the clock for a 14-10 upset win.: Smith with Grizzard, p. 7.
39 "I was absolutely too heavy . . . where I just wasn't enjoying tennis.": Scott M. Reid, "Wicked Return by Lettiere," *The Atlanta Journal/The Atlanta Constitution*, May 13, 1994, p. D4.
39 "It let me fall in love . . . really do like playing the game.": Reid, "Wicked Return."
39 "I really do believe the injury was a blessing,": Reid, "Wicked Return."
40 Bob Hope, Errol Flynn, . . . hobnobbed with them all.: Outlar, p. 74.
40 That's where they met fellow passenger . . . and refused to leave.: Outlar, p. 73.
40 The peeved starlet . . . strictly forbidding any drinking.: Outlar, p. 74.
41 Freshman Mike Cavan was sitting . . . Cavan replied, "My dad.": Barnhart, *What It Means*, p. 77.
41 Cavan even went to his mother . . . still miss him a whole lot.": Barnhart, *What It Means*, p. 77.
41 In December 1966, Cavan . . . had made for me.": Barnhart, *What It Means*, p. 76.
42 "were an experienced team, but we . . . is always the first one.": Hix, *Hoop Tales*, p. 37.
42 Georgia led 50-41 . . . as the clock ticked away.: Hix, *Hoop Tales*, p. 38.
42 Banks improvised. . . . before deciding to fall in.: Hix, *Hoop Tales*, p. 39.
43 The Tennessee coaches made a strategic . . . strode into Scott's bedroom.: Smith with Grizzard, p. 64.
43 Scott wanted to sign with Georgia, . . . go to the University of Georgia.": Smith with Grizzard, p. 65.
44 "such an epidemic of Southern hospitality . . . instead of the beloved red and black.": Outlar, p. 11.
44 "hundreds of flags waved welcome . . . the Mason and Dixon line.": Outlar, p. 11.
44 The Yale team, the band . . . "Glory, Glory" to old Georgia.: Hix, *Stadium Stories*, p. 112.
45 "You'll never do anything at Georgia. There's no support there.": Yoculan and Donaldson, p. 14.
45 The athletic department was discussing eliminating the program.: Yoculan and Donaldson, p. 4.
45 routinely drew fewer than 200 . . . boyfriends, roommates, and families.": Yoculan and Donaldson, p. 4.
45 The women shared practice space . . . physical education building: Yoculan and Donaldson, p. 6.
45 Yoculan's office was a cubicle . . . they couldn't hear her: Yoculan and Donaldson, p. 7.
45 "To me, it was wonderful," . . . when I first came here.": Yoculan and Donaldson, p. 8.
46 In high school, though, Anderson . . . just wasn't a fair comparison,": Barnhart, *What It Means*, pp. 238-39.
46 A long way from home . . . opener against Tennessee: Barnhart, *What It Means*, p. 239.
46 He left town . . . "It's a good thing I did.": Barnhart, *What It*

Means, p. 240.

47 the "Mercer boys came in . . . the line of the Macon and Northern.": Stegeman, p. 5.

47 the pre-game festivities included . . . quite a ripple of laughter.": Stegeman, p. 5.

47 After the 50-0 Georgia win, . . . Even the goat was ridden.": Stegeman, p. 7.

47 the "mascot goat will be along . . . the paraphernalia of the football team.": Stegeman, p. 8.

47 a black coat or blanket . . . "U" and "G" -- on each side: Magill, p. 175.

47 and a hat with . . . goat was "enthusiastically applauded.": Stegeman, p. 11.

47 A couple of seasons later . . . owned by a student,: Magill, p. 175.

48 "I have never really been able . . . you might say even scary.": Jim Klobuchar and Fran Tarkenton, "The Quarterback," *Echoes of Georgia Football*, p. 66.

48 "was the first in a long line . . . "a reasonable chance of lettering at Georgia, eventually.": Klobuchar and Tarkenton, p. 64.

48 Bill Herron in the left corner . . . game-winning play in the huddle.: Barnhart, *What It Means*, p. 64.

48 "All the first-rate college quarterbacks . . . were automatic first-round choices.": Klobuchar and Tarkenton, p. 69.

48 "I think you're the best quarterback in football today.": Barnhart, *What It Means*, p. 65

49 Georgia lost the SEC title . . . national championship with a 2-1 win.: "Miracle!" georgiadogs.com: Baseball: 1990 National Champions, http://admin.xosn.com/ViewArticle.dbml?DB_OEM_ID8800&ATCLID=319082.

50 He got his nickname . . . Ocmulgee River catfish.: Magill, p. 21.

50 Georgia's star center, Bill Strickland, . . . to shoot the free throws,: Magill, p. 21.

51 Kelly Miller – Georgia's first two-time . . . she would get down there,": Wendy Parker, "Last Call for Miller Time," *The Atlanta Journal/The Atlanta Constitution*, March 1, 2001, p. E1.

51 "It's kind of freaky, I guess,": Parker, "Last Call."

51 "I can't imagine ever playing without Kelly,": Parker, "Last Call."

52 Dooley and Eaves agreed that . . . previous ties to Georgia.: Hix, Stadium Stories, p. 34.

52 Dooley didn't exactly run up . . . 'Hey, Vince, how 'bout a job?'": Hix, *Stadium Stories*, p. 36.

52 the best hire Dooley . . . "coaching staff for seventeen years.": Hix, *Stadium Stories*, p. 4.

53 "That guy Spankovich is at it . . . " freshman game at Grant Field.: Marc Lancaster, "No. 3: University of Georgia Athlete of the Century: Frank Sinkwich," *Echoes of Georgia Football*, p. 49.

53 A magazine article in the 1950s . . . to back up its point.: Lancaster, "No. 3," p. 54.

53 "Through his performances in . . . Georgia football for the first time.": Lancaster, "No. 3," p. 53.

53 "He put us on the map," Dan Magill said.: Lancaster, "No. 3," p. 54.

54 "gobbled up innings and wins . . . the person out there.": Chip Towers, "Green Alone Makes Dogs' Staff Deep, " *The Atlanta Journal/The Atlanta Constitution*, May 27, 2005, p. D9.

54 "We just have a tendency . . . this seems to be working,": Towers, "Green

Alone."
54 I think God made it simple. Just accept him and believe.: Bettinger, p. 47.
55 They first showed up in 1929,: Sharpe, p. 35.
55 They did so on Oct. 27, 2007, . . . bell was returned to its post.: "Georgia Traditions: The Chapel Bell," http://www/georgiadogs.com/ViewArticle.dbml?DB_OEM_ID=8800&KEY=&ATCLID, April 3, 2009.
55 It's gonna be sad not . . . warm feeling at the same time.: Sharpe, p. 35.
56 The two teams played at . . . and a high fence.: Stegeman, p. 71.
56 His punt struck the goal posts . . . a search of several minutes: Stegeman, p. 72.
56 did the Techster find the ball . . . finally know what had happened.: Stegeman, p. 73.
57 The Detroit Pistons pursued Wilkins hard, . . .committed to staying at Georgia.": Hix, *Hoop Tales*, p. 16.
57 He loved being at Georgia too much to leave it yet.: Hix, *Hoop Tales*, p. 17.
58 Howard "Smiley" Johnson came to Georgia . . . and lettered for three seasons.: Magill, pp. 35-36.
58 He received his nickname . . . the Japanese struck on Dec. 7.: Magill, p. 37.
58 he didn't cuss, smoke, or drink, and he read the Bible every night.: Magill, p. 37.
58 so impressive in his officer . . . a Gold Star for his action.: Magill, p. 38.
59 He told offensive coordinator . . . "to let him carry the ball.": Smith with Grizzard, p. 87.
59 "with a full head of steam, . . . stretched out on the Tartan turf.": Smith with Grizzard, pp. 87-88.
59 "I don't think anybody . . . of what was to come": Smith with Grizzard, p. 89.
60 Growing up, he spent . . . and signed Towns to a scholarship.: Karen Rosen, "Legend as an Athlete and Coach," *The Atlanta Journal/The Atlanta Constitution*, April 10, 1991, p. F9.
60 Vince Dooley said one of his . . . inscribed on a huge plaque.: Rosen.
60 Mel Rosen, coach of . . . "track athlete Georgia ever had.": Rosen.
61 "There will be no more football at the university.": Stegeman, p. 42.
61 Doctors at the game realized . . . him to Grady Hospital.: Stegeman, p. 41.
61 Gammon died before sunrise. . . . disbanded their football teams.: Stegeman, p. 42.
61 He wrote an open letter . . . rather than football's abolition.: Stegeman, p. 43.
61 "It would be inexpressibly sad . . . cherished object of his life..": Outlar, p. 26.
62 the family had no money . . . "I'll break the other one.": Loran Smith, "Trippi Successful On and Off the Field," *Echoes of Georgia Football*, p. 59.
62 But the local high school coach . . . his football footwear. Smith, "Trippi Successful," pp. 59-60.
62 He was the punter until . . . I would sign with Georgia.": Smith, "Trippi Successful, p. 60.
62 "I had promised coach . . . never regretted the decision.": Outlar, p. 82.
63 This was after Coach Andy Landers . . . he was recruiting Stacey Ford,: Ailene Voisin, "Roundtree Helps Awaken Lady Dogs' Potential," *The Atlanta Journal/The Atlanta Constitution*, Jan. 10, 1995, p. B2.
63 Devastated, Roundtree considered going to work and forgetting about college basketball,: Ailene Voisin, "Nurtured in a Small Texas Town, Roundtree Develops into Top Dog," *The Atlanta Journal/*

The Atlanta Constitution, March 25, 1996, p. D7.

63 "That's it. I won't go anywhere.": Voisin, "Roundtree Helps Awaken."

63 Accustomed to being playing with . . . Blaylock didn't have much to offer her: Voisin, "Roundtree Helps Awaken."

63 She countered that perhaps . . . told Blaylock to send the papers: Voisin, "Roundtree Helps Awaken."

64 "the greatest defensive player I ever coached,": Dooley with Smith, p. 123.

64 Coaches Bill Lewis and Steve Greer . . . the classroom was a snap.": Dooley with Smith, p. 123.

64 "When it came to the big play, . . . overall ability and performance.": Dooley with Smith, p. 123.

65 Vince Dooley once called Stanfill . . . range, quickness, and competiveness.": "Bill Stanfill," *Wikipedia.*

65 He suffered four fused disks in his neck:: Barnhart, p. 146.

65 a problem that began . . . exhibition game in 1975: "Bill Stanfill," *Wikipedia.*

65 and a bad disc in his lower back.: Barnhart, p. 146.

65 He was in such pain . . . three surgeries to correct the problem.: "Bill Stanfill," *Wikipedia.*

65 He had both hips replaced . . . I loved going to Georgia.": Barnhart, p. 146.

66 He had some offers . . . McAuley didn't get to play much,": Chip Towers, "Captain Courageous," *The Atlanta Journal/The Atlanta Constitution*, March 5, 2006, p. D6.

66 "It's a great honor, and . . . I just love Georgia basketball.": Towers, "Captain Courageous."

67 "he might just be . . . history of Georgia sports.": Hix, *Stadium Stories*, p. 150.

67 "has achieved an exalted status in the lore of Georgia football,": Hix, *Stadium Stories*, p. 150.

67 "were slow to embrace Munson the outsider.": Hix, *Stadium Stories*, p. 151.

67 "He wasn't part of the team . . . totally impartial, cold, dry.": Hix, *Stadium Stories*, p. 152.

67 That all changed in November . . . "WE'VE just beaten Tennessee!": Hix, Stadium Stories, p. 162.

68 back in the summer of '64 . . . two-time All-America at Georgia: Magill, p. 137.

68 Dooley claimed "football knee" in not playing tennis again: Magill, p. 138.

69 "I went through . . . history of Georgia football.": Barnhart, *"What It Means,"* p. 315.

69 "a tough transition" . . . "a beleaguered football team.": Barnhart, *What It Means*, p. 316.

69 "A lot of strange things . . . all went against us.": Barnhart, What It Means, p. 318.

69 "I wouldn't trade anything . . . lucky to be a part of [Georgia football].": Barnhart, *What It Means*, p. 318.

70 Doctors said he would never . . . the team as its manager.: Magill, p. 69.

70 He spent his freshman year . . . his sophomore season.: Magill, p. 69.

70 On the bus ride from Athens . . . going to break the drought.": Gene Asher, "The Man Who Broke the Drought," *Echoes of Georgia Football*, pp. 18-19.

70 Sapp recovered a Tech fumble . . . nine times on the subsequent drive: Magill, p. 69.

70 After quarterback Charlie Britt . . . from the one, he scored: Asher, p. 17.

70 "did as much for Georgia pride . . . anyone in Bulldogs history.": Asher, p. 17.
71 "People started lining up at 4:30 in the afternoon on game day": Hix, *Stadium Stories*, p. 84.
71 a full month after other prospects had announced their choice: Hix, Stadium Stories, p. 85.
71 Herschel chose Southern California, . . . the first outside the family to know: Smith with Grizzard, p. 74.
72 "Making the transition . . . that you're out there.": Hix, *Hoop Tales*, p. 160.
72 His career average per . . . still the Georgia record,: Hix, *Hoop Tales*, p. 160.
72 he averaged nearly ten yards every time he touched the football: Hix, *Hoop Tales*, p. 159.
72 Drafted by pro football's . . . of basketball eligibility left.: Hix, *Hoop Tales*, p. 165.
73 Bobby Thompson intercepted a pass . . . Georgia led 7-0.: Cromartie, p. 310.
73 Georgia went 97 yards in two plays. . . . true again on the extra point.: Cromartie, p. 311.
73 Al Pollard plowed in . . . running only twelve plays.: Cromartie, p. 312.
73 Georgia's first-ever 40-point lead over Tech: Cromartie, p. 313.
73 One writer tagged him "St. Vincent the Merciful.": Cromartie, p. 309.
74 That evening the Georgia fans . . . Yellow River trestle west of Lawrenceville.: Stegeman, p. 55.
74 After the train had "plunged . . . who were soon in an uproar.: Stegeman, p. 56.
74 They rushed the captives and . . . . some immediate form of justice.": Stegeman, pp. 56-57.
74 But the tracks were repaired, . . . an exciting story to tell.: Stegeman, p. 57.
75 Twins Jonas and Jarvis Hayes are so close . . . into the locker room and saw him.": Hix, *Hoop Tales*, p. 95.
75 Out of high school, they insisted . . . to both of them: Hix, *Hoop Tales*, p. 99.
75 Only three schools . . . agreed to take them both,: Hix, *Hoop Tales*, p. 97.
75 "I've got these two sons . . . want to come home.": Hix, *Hoop Tales*, p. 94.
75 "You just instill things . . . and you will go far.": Hix, *Hoop Tales*, p. 111.
76 Offensive coordinator Bill Pace told . . . Clark thought of quitting.: Barnhart, *What It Means*, p. 160.
76 defensive coordinator Erk Russell approached . . . I wanted to play.": Barnhart, *What It Means*, p. 160.
77 Prior to the final home meet . . . a pristine practice space with 16,000 square feet.: Peter Cox, "Yoculan's Athens Farewell Brings Back Memories," *The Atlanta Journal-Constitution*, March 13, 2009, http://www.ajc.com/sports/content/sorts/uga/stories/2009/03/13/uga_gymnastics_suzanne, March 13, 2009.
78 "to bring stability to a sports program that was in tatters": Hix, *Stadium Stories*, p. 30.
78 The next morning, Vince Dooley . . . on a plane to Athens.: Hix, *Stadium Stories*, p. 32.
78 "I could have walked" . . . the downtown Holiday Inn: Hix, *Stadium Stories*, p. 33.
78 Dooley was so unknown that . . . "our fine young coach.": Hix, Stadium Stories, p. 34.
78 He had received . . . not the newspapers: Hix, *Stadium Stories*, p. 33.

79 "With no less than . . . tennis players only dream": Tony Barnhart, "Sheppard's Comeback Lets UGA Avoid Huge Deficit," *The Atlanta Journal/The Atlanta Constitution*, May 18, 1994, p. G8.

79 "You never give up until . . . "It was big. Really big,": Barnhart, "Sheppard's Comeback."

80 He considered transferring, but decided . . . start anywhere else.: Lee Shearer, "D.J. Shockley: Quarterback Earns Respect," *Echoes of Georgia Football*, p. 103.

80 "He waited patiently, . . . or anything like that Shearer, p. 104.

80 Offensive coordinator Neil Callaway said . . . on our whole football team.": Shearer, p. 105.

81 Since 1981 when the NCAA . . . fourth in the country in total wins during that time: "Georgia Biographies: Andy Landers," georgiadogs.com: Women's Basketball: History, http://www.georgiadogs.com/ViewArticle.dbml? SPSID=46833&SPID=3594&DB_OEM, Oct. 29, 2007.

81 They have averaged about 24 . . . in more than half of the AP polls: "Georgia Biographies: Andy Landers."

81 "She put our program on the map . . . gave us the credibility": Scott M. Reid, "Georgia Cornerstone Harris Will Have Her Jersey Retired," *The Atlanta Journal/The Atlanta Constitution*, Feb. 28, 1993, p. D7.

81 "We do not choose . . . the foundation on which we stand.": R. Alan Culpepper, "The Gospel of Luke: Introduction, Commentary, and Reflections," *The New Interpreter's Bible* (Nashville: Abingdon Press, 1995) Vol. IX, p. 153.

82 Academic counselor Curt Fludd caught . . . against Tennessee was a miracle.: Smith with Grizzard, pp. 114, 116.

82 In the end zone, Scott shouted, . . . but now I was back.": Smith with Grizzard, p. 156.

83 when he was the only returning . . . a whole team in himself.": Stegeman, p. 63.

83 "a good fist-fight was an integral . . . shy away from anyone.": Stegeman, p. 61.

83 In the 1903 game against . . . arrested and hauled downtown.: Stegeman, p. 66.

84 At the 1991 conference championships . . . that came with the fall.: Yoculan and Donaldson, pp. 29-30.

84 Coach Suzanne Yoculan said she was never sure . . . "minimize stress on the broken toe.": Yoculan and Donaldson, p. 30.

84 Her teammates fidgeted, . . . she nailed a 9.45.: Yoculan and Donaldson, p. 30.

84 "This is the happiest moment of my life,": Yoculan with Donaldson, p. 30.

85 In the spring of 1928 . . . The boy's name was Spurgeon Chandler.: Magill, p. 18.

85 Chandler starred as the left . . . arm problems forced his retirement.: Magill, 20.

86 Wally Butts, who took over . . . resurrected the silver britches in 1980: "Silver Britches," georgiadogs.com: History: Georgia Traditions, http://www.georgiadogs.com/ViewArticle.dbml?DB_OEM_ID=8800&KEY=&ATCLID, Oct. 16, 2007.

86 He discussed with his staff . . . appearance in the first game of 1964.: "The Georgia 'G Helmet," georgiadogs.com: History: Georgia Traditions, http://www.georgiadogs.com/ViewArticle.dbml/DB_OEM_ID=8800&KEY=&ATCLID, Oct. 16, 2007.

86 Uga's jerseys are custom-made . . . . His old ones are destroyed: "Mascot," georgiadogs.com: History: Georgia Traditions, http://www.georgiadogs.com/

ViewArticle.dbml?&SPSID48586&SPID, Oct. 16, 2007.

87 "academic performance fairly dwarfed . . . becoming an orthopedic surgeon,: Hix, *Hoop Tales*, p. 114.

87 upon the advice of his . . . a medical student well: Hix, *Hoop Tales*, p. 122.

87 "a symbol, not just . . . good about college athletics": Hix, *Hoop Tales*, p. 126.

87 "Never before had Georgia . . ." both basketball and the classroom.: Hix, *Hoop Tales*, p. 129.

87 "I can honestly say . . . study for six straight hours.": Hix, *Hoop Tales*, p. 126.

88 Dooley simply looked at Butler and said, "Field goal.": Barnhart, *What It Means*, p. 246.

88 the decision "freaked out the people in the stands.": Barnhart, *What It Means*, p. 246.

88 "So we'll try to kick one . . . plus a foot and a half!": Barnhart, *What It Means*, p. 358.

88 "And Butler kicked a long one . . . believe what he did!": Barnhart, *What It Means*, p. 358.

88 "I knew it was going . . . and dropped to his knee: Barnhart, What It Means, p. 246.

88 the game Bulldog fans voted the greatest game ever played in Sanford Stadium: Alex Crevar, "Kicking Down the Door," *Echoes of Georgia Football*, p. 91.

89 He was a graduate assistant . . . "succeeding in whatever I do": Brian Curtis, "Faith in the Game," *Echoes of Georgia Football*, p. 136.

89 "If [players] come to me, . . . force [my faith] on anyone": Curtis, p. 137.

89 "He maintains a steady, emotional . . . on the task at hand,": Curtis, p. 137.

89 "open about faith. That a man of God is running the program.": Curtis, p. 137.

90 In May 1919, in a game . . . Satterfield struck out the last two batters: Cromartie, p. 86.

90 The Tech "stunt" and the . . . all afternoon and into the night: Cromartie, pp. 86-87.

90 Tommy Philpot then embarrassed Tech . . . "the former German Kaiser should be hung.": Cromartie, p. 87.

BIBLIOGRAPHY

"All Americans." georgiadogs.com: Football: History: Honors and Awards. http://admin.xosn.attachments1/1581.pdf?SPSID=46724&SPSID.

Arey, Norman. "Georgia Names Tennis Complex for Dan Magill." *The Atlanta Journal/The Atlanta Constitution*. 14 May 1993. E3.

Asher, Gene. "The Man Who Broke the Drought." *Echoes of Georgia Football: The Greatest Stories Ever Told*. Ed. Ken Samelson. Chicago: Triumph Books, 2006. 17-19.

Barnhart, Tony. "Sheppard's Comeback Lets UGA Avoid Huge Deficit." *The Atlanta Journal/The Atlanta Constitution*. 18 May 1994. G8.

---. *What It Means to Be a Bulldog: Vince Dooley, Mark Richt, and Georgia's Greatest Players*. Chicago: Triumph Books, 2004.

Bettinger, Jim & Julie S. *The Book of Bowden*. Nashville: TowleHouse Publishing, 2001.

"Bill Stanfill." *Wikipedia, the free encyclopedia*. http:en.wikipedia.org/wiki/Bill_Stanfill. 22 Aug. 2007.

Bolton, Clyde. *The Crimson Tide: A Story of Alabama Football*. Huntsville, AL: The Strode Publishers, 1972.

-----. *War Eagle: A Story of Auburn Football*. Huntsville, AL: The Strode Publishers, 1973.

Clemons, J.C. "No. 24 Georgia Women Miss NCAA Field of 48." *The Atlanta Journal/The Atlanta Constitution*. 16 March 1992. E1.

Cox, Peter. "Yoculan's Athens Farewell Brings Back Memories." *The Atlanta Journal/The Atlanta Constitution*. 13 March 2009. http:www.ajc.com/sports/content/sports/uga/stories/2009/03/13/uga_gymnastics_suzanne.

Crevar, Alex. "Kicking Down the Door." *Echoes of Georgia Football: The Greatest Stories Ever Told*. Ed. Ken Samelson. Chicago: Triumph Books, 2006. 91-93.

Cromartie, Bill. *Clean Old-Fashioned Hate*. Huntsville, AL: The Strode Publishers, 1977.

Culpepper, R. Alan. "The Gospel of Luke: Introduction, Commentary, and Reflections." *The New Interpreter's Bible*. Nashville: Abingdon Press, 1995. Vol. IX. 1-490.

Curtis, Brian. "Faith in the Game." *Echoes of Georgia Football: The Greatest Stories Ever Told*. Ed. Ken Samelson. Chicago: Triumph Books, 2006. 133-152.

Dooley, Vince with Blake Giles. "1980: The Pig." *Echoes of Georgia Football: The Greatest Stories Ever Told*. Ed. Ken Samelson. Chicago: Triumph Books, 2006. 161-68.

Dooley, Vince with Loran Smith. *Dooley's Dawgs: 40 Years of Championship Athletics at the University of Georgia*. Atlanta: Longstreet Press, 2003.

"Georgia Biographies: Andy Landers." georgiadogs.com: Women's Baskketball: History. http://www.georgiadogs.com/ViewArticle.dmbl?SPSID=46833&SPID=3594&DB_OEM. 29 Oct. 2007.

"Georgia Biographies: Kelley Hester." georgiadogs.com: Women's Golf: Coaches. http://www.georgiadogs.com/ViewArticle.dbml?SPSID=40683&SPID=3578&DB_OEM. 14 Aug. 2007.

"The Georgia 'G' Helmet." georgiadogs.com: History: Georgia Traditions. http://www.georgiadogs.com/ViewArticle.dmbl?DB_OEM_ID=8800&KEY=&ATCLID. 16 Oct. 2007.

"Georgia Traditions: The Chapel Bell." http://www.georgiadogs.com/ViewArticle.dbml?DB_OEM_ID=8800&KEY=&ATCLID.

"The History of the University of Georgia Redcoat Band 1905-2005." http://bands.music.uga.edu/redcoats/history.php.

Hix, Tim. *Hoop Tales: Georgia Bulldogs Men's Basketball*. Guilford, CN: The Globe Pequot Press, 2006.

-----. *Stadium Stories: Georgia Bulldogs: Great Moments in Team History*. Guilford, CN: The Globe Pequot Press, 2006.

Hummer, Steve. "Lycett's Long, Strange Trip Nears an End." *The Atlanta Journal/The Atlanta Constitution*. 29 March 2003. E8.

Johnson, Troy. "Senior Class Creates Lasting Memories." http://www.onlineathens.com/1996/120196/1201.senior.html. 19 Aug. 2003.

Kendall, Josh. "Defensive Coaches Braced for Penalty." *The Telegraph*. 28 Oct. 2007. 4C.

-----. "Moreno, Teammates Mount Day-Long Georgia Celebration." *The Telegraph*. 28 Oct. 2007. 1C.

Kindred, Dave. "Germ Study a Model Role for Volleyball 'Gym Rat.'" *The Atlanta Journal/The Atlanta Constitution*. 21 Jan. 1996. E3.

Klobuchar, Jim, and Fran Tarkenton. "The Quarterback." *Echoes of Georgia Football: The Greatest Stories Ever Told*. Ed. Ken Samelson. Chicago: Triumph Books, 2006. 63-70.

Lancaster, Marc. "Bobo, Edwards Rally Dogs." http://www.onlineathens.com/1996/111796/1117.rally.html. 14 Aug. 2003.

-----. "No. 3: University of Georgia Athlete of the Century: Frank Sinkwich." *Echoes of Georgia Football: The Greatest Stories Ever Told*. Ed. Ken Samelson. Chicago: Triumph Books, 2006. 47-55.

Lough, Michael A. "Two Paths, One Hometown." *The Telegraph*. 6 Aug. 2007. 1C.

Magill, Dan. *Dan Magill's Bull-Doggerel: Fifty Years of Anecdotes from the Greatest Bulldog Ever*. Atlanta: Longstreet Press, 1993.

Manuel, Marion and Scott M. Reid. "Georgia Rejects NWIT; Tech Jumps at Invitation." *The Atlanta Journal/The Atlanta Constitution*. 16 March 1992. E4.

"Mascot." georgiadogs.com: History: Georgia Traditions. http://www.georgiadogs.com/ViewArticle.dbml?&SPSID48586&SPID. 16 Oct. 2007.

"Miracle!" georgiadogs.com: Baseball: 1990 National Champions. http://admin/xosn.com/ViewArticle.dbml?DB_OEM_ID=8800&ATCLID=319082. 16 Oct. 2007.

Outlar, Jesse. *Between the Hedges: A Story of Georgia Football*. Huntsville, AL: The Strode Publishers, 1974.

Parker, Wendy. "Last Call for Miller Time." *The Atlanta Journal/The Atlanta Constitution*. 1 March 2001. E1.

---. "Soccer Gets Kick-Start at Georgia." *The Atlanta Journal/The Atlanta Constitution*. 1 Sept. 1995. E1.

Reid, Scott M. "Georgia Cornerstone Harris Will Have Her Jersey Retired." *The Atlanta Journal/The Atlanta Constitution*. 28 Feb, 1993. D7.

-----. "Georgia's McGuire Leaving Ailments and Anger Behind." *The Atlanta Journal/The Atlanta Constitution*. 13 May 1993. G1.

---. "Wicked Return by Lettiere." *The Atlanta Journal/The Atlanta Constitution*. 13 May 1994. D4.

Rosen, Karen. "Legend as an Athlete and Coach: 34-Year Coaching Tenure Longest at UGA." *The Atlanta Journal/The Atlanta Constitution*. 10 April 1991. F9.

Schlabach, Mark. "Lady Dogs Top Panthers 4-0 in Debut." *The Atlanta Journal/The Atlanta Constitution*. 4 Sept. 1995. D2.

Sharpe, Wilton. *Bulldog Madness: Great Eras in Georgia Football*. Nashville: Cumberland House, 2005.

Shearer, Lee. "D.J. Shockley: Quarterback Earns Respect." *Echoes of*

Georgia Football: The Greatest Stories Ever Told. Ed. Ken Samelson. Chicago: Triumph Books, 2006. 103-105.

"Silver Britches." georgiadogs.com: Georgia Traditions: History. http://wwwgeorgiadogs.com/ViewArticle.dbml?DB_OEM_ID=8800&KEY=&ATCLID. 16 Oct. 2007.

Smith, Loran. "Trippi Successful On and Off the Field." *Echoes of Georgia Football: The Greatest Stories Ever Told*. Ed. Ken Samelson. Chicago: Triumph Books, 2006. 57-62.

Smith, Loran with Lewis Grizzard. *Glory! Glory! Georgia's 1980 Championship Season: The Inside Story*. Atlanta: Peachtree Publishers Limited, 1981.

Stegeman, John F. *The Ghosts of Herty Field: Early Days on a Southern Gridiron*. Athens: The University of Georgia Press, 1997.

Towers, Chip. "Bobo, Edwards Sparkle in Four-Overtime Victory." *The Augusta Chronicle*. 17 Nov. 1996. http://chronicle.augusta.com/stories/111796.georgia.html.

---. "Captain Courageous: Senior Walk-On Gets His Due." *The Atlanta Journal/The Atlanta Constitution*. 5 March 2006. D6.

---. "Green Alone Makes Dogs' Staff Deep." *The Atlanta Journal/The Atlanta Constitution*. 27 May 2005. D9.

---. "Redemption: Bobo, Edwards Lead Dogs to 4-OT Win." http://www.onlineathens.com/1996/111796/1117.dogs.html.

Voisin, Ailene. "NCAA Bubble Bursts for Tournament Heroines Tech, Georgia." *The Atlanta Journal/The Atlanta Constitution*. 16 March 1992. E5.

---. "Nurtured in a Small Texas Town, Roundtree Develops into Top Dog." *The Atlanta Journal/The Atlanta Constitution*. 25 March 1996. D7.

---. "Roundtree Helps Awaken Lady Dogs' Potential." *The Atlanta Journal/The Atlanta Constitution*. 10 Jan. 1995. B2.

Wilkinson, Jack. "On the Track, Lady Dogs Find Common Ground." *The Atlanta Journal/The Atlanta Constitution*. 2 June 1995. E6.

Wodraska, Lya. "No Skirting the Issue at UGA." *The Atlanta Journal/The Atlanta Constitution*. 20 Jan. 1993. F7.

Yoculan, Suzanne and Bill Donaldson. *Perfect 10: The University of Georgia Gymdogs and the Rise of Women's College Gymnastics in America*. Athens: Hill Street Press LLC, 2006.

INDEX

(by devotion number)

GEORGIA